"Anderson's insights... continue to influence Google's strategic thinking in a profound way."

-Eric Schmidt, CEO, Google

"Anyone who cares about media...
must read this book."

-Rob Glaser, CEO, RealNetworks

"I'd put Anderson and his work on par with Malcolm Gladwell and Clayton M. Christensen as one of the more important pieces of business philosophy published in the emerging global, digital era."

-Alan T. Saracevic, *San Francisco Chronicle*

The Long Tail

from SmarterComics™

by **Chris Anderson**

Illustrated by **Shane Clester**

Adapted by Cullen Bunn

Executive Editor
Corey Michael Blake

Creative Director
Nathan Brown

Comic book cover design based on the original artwork by Scott Dadich

rtc
A Round Table Companies Production
www.roundtablepress.com

Foreword

This book brings my life so much happiness. Finally I can read *The Long Tail*. I'm part of a small niche of entrepreneurs that reads way more comic books than business books. And the coolest part about it all is that's what this book is all about! We are coming out of an age where everything was mass produced, where we were told what we were supposed to like and our culture was driven by a small number of mainstream hits. Not anymore...

Chris Anderson is a visionary. He first spoke of *The Long Tail* in 2004, and his concepts have only become more and more relevant since then. Chris also gives some great real world advice in the book on how to cater to the long tail. In my own crowdsourcing t-shirt business, Threadless.com, we work with tens of thousands of artists around the world. The whole way we do business is very much in line with the concepts in this book. Anyone can produce and distribute products. All of the power is in the hands of the creators and the stories all come from the community, not from the business.

I for one am happy to be living in this new culture of the long tail where I can finally learn a little business savvy in the magical comic book format. Maybe eventually I'll even be able to read it in waterproof form in the bathtub, another small niche group I belong to.

Jake Nickell
Founder, Threadless.com

The Long Tail

from SmarterComics™

THE TRACKING OF TOP-SELLER LISTS IS A NATIONAL OBSESSION.

OUR CULTURE IS A MASSIVE POPULARITY CONTEST. WE ARE CONSUMED BY HITS—MAKING THEM, CHOOSING THEM, TALKING ABOUT THEM, AND FOLLOWING THEIR RISE AND FALL.

THIS IS THE WORLD THE BLOCKBUSTER BUILT.

THE MASSIVE MEDIA AND ENTERTAINMENT INDUSTRIES GREW UP OVER THE PAST HALF CENTURY ON THE BACK OF BOX-OFFICE ROCKETS, GOLD RECORDS, AND DOUBLE-DIGIT TV RATINGS.

THE STAR-MAKING SYSTEM THAT HOLLYWOOD BEGAN EIGHT DECADES AGO HAS NOW SPUN OUT INTO EVERY CORNER OF COMMERCE, FROM SHOES TO CHEFS.

HITS, IN SHORT, RULE.

YET LOOK A LITTLE CLOSER AND YOU'LL SEE THAT THIS PICTURE, WHICH FIRST EMERGED WITH THE POSTWAR BROADCAST ERA OF RADIO AND TELEVISION, IS NOW STARTING TO TATTER AT THE EDGES.

HITS ARE STARTING TO—GASP!—RULE LESS.

NUMBER ONE IS STILL NUMBER ONE, BUT THE SALES THAT GO WITH THAT ARE NOT WHAT THEY ONCE WERE.

1

MOST OF THE TOP FIFTY BEST-SELLING ALBUMS OF ALL TIME WERE RECORDED IN THE SEVENTIES AND EIGHTIES.

HOLLYWOOD BOX-OFFICE REVENUE WAS DOWN BY MORE THAN 6 PERCENT IN 2005.

EVERY YEAR NETWORK TV LOSES MORE OF ITS AUDIENCE TO HUNDREDS OF NICHE CABLE CHANNELS.

IN SHORT, ALTHOUGH WE STILL OBSESS OVER HITS, THEY ARE NOT QUITE THE ECONOMIC FORCE THEY ONCE WERE. WHERE ARE THOSE FICKLE CONSUMERS GOING INSTEAD?

THEY ARE SCATTERED TO THE WINDS AS MARKETS FRAGMENT INTO COUNTLESS NICHES. THE ONE BIG GROWTH AREA IS THE WEB, BUT IT IS AN UNCATEGORIZABLE SEA OF A MILLION DESTINATIONS, EACH DEFYING IN ITS OWN WAY THE CONVENTIONAL LOGIC OF MEDIA AND MARKETING.

I CAME OF AGE IN THE PEAK OF THE MASS-CULTURE ERA—THE SEVENTIES AND EIGHTIES. THE AVERAGE TEENAGER THEN HAD ACCESS TO A HALF DOZEN TV CHANNELS.

THERE WERE THREE OR FOUR ROCK RADIO STATIONS IN ANY TOWN THAT LARGELY DICTATED WHAT MUSIC PEOPLE LISTENED TO. ONLY A FEW LUCKY KIDS WITH MONEY BUILT RECORD COLLECTIONS THAT VENTURED FARTHER AFIELD.

BOOKS

RETURN OF THE JEDI

GODZILLA

TEENAGE ME

RECORD PLAYER

ANALOG TV

COMICS

WE ALL SAW THE SAME SUMMER BLOCKBUSTERS IN THE THEATER AND GOT OUR NEWS FROM THE SAME PAPERS AND BROADCASTS.

ABOUT THE ONLY PLACES YOU COULD EXPLORE OUTSIDE THE MAINSTREAM WERE THE LIBRARY AND THE COMIC BOOK SHOPS.

CONTRAST MY ADOLESCENCE WITH THAT OF BEN, A SIXTEEN-YEAR-OLD WHO GREW UP WITH THE INTERNET.

WI FI

PS3   PSP

X BOX 360

DIGITAL TV

PRINTER/SCANNER

TYPICAL TEENAGER

IPAD

IPOD

MAC BOOK

HE'S GOT A MAC IN HIS BEDROOM, A FULLY STOCKED IPOD (AND A WEEKLY ITUNES ALLOWANCE) AND A POSSE OF FRIENDS WITH THE SAME.

LIKE THE REST OF HIS TEENAGE FRIENDS, BEN HAS NEVER KNOWN A WORLD WITHOUT BROADBAND, CELL PHONES, MP3'S, TIVO, AND ONLINE SHOPPING.

3

THE MAIN EFFECT OF ALL THIS CONNECTIVITY IS UNLIMITED AND UNFILTERED ACCESS TO CULTURE AND CONTENT OF ALL SORTS.

FROM BEN'S PERSPECTIVE, THE CULTURAL LANDSCAPE IS A SEAMLESS CONTINUUM FROM HIGH TO LOW, WITH COMMERCIAL AND AMATEUR CONTENT COMPETING EQUALLY FOR HIS ATTENTION.

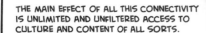

HOLLYWOOD
TIVO
SIRIUS
FAN FILMS
FANFIC
BLIP.FM
WEBCOMICS
NETFLIX
ITUNES
COMICS

YouTUBE
WARLORD: OFFICIAL MOVIE TRAILER

HE SIMPLY DOESN'T DISTINGUISH BETWEEN MAINSTREAM HITS AND UNDERGROUND NICHES — HE PICKS WHAT HE LIKES FROM AN INFINITE MENU WHERE HOLLYWOOD MOVIES AND AMATEUR VIDEOS ARE LISTED SIDE BY SIDE.

BEN WATCHES JUST TWO HOURS OR SO A WEEK OF REGULAR TV, MOSTLY WEST WING (TIME SHIFTED, OF COURSE) AND FIREFLY, A CANCELED SPACE SERIAL HE HAS STORED ON HIS TIVO.

HE ALSO COUNTS AS TV THE ANIME HE DOWNLOADS WITH BITTORRENT, A PEER-TO-PEER FILESHARING TECHNOLOGY, BECAUSE IT WAS ORIGINALLY BROADCAST ON JAPANESE TELEVISION.

WHEN IT COMES TO MOVIES, STAR WARS IS A PASSION, AS WAS THE MATRIX SERIES.

BUT HE ALSO WATCHES MOVIES HE DOWNLOADS, SUCH AS AMATEUR MACHINIMA (MOVIES MADE BY CONTROLLING CHARACTERS IN VIDEO GAMES) AND INDEPENDENT PRODUCTIONS.

$41.00
HAN SHOT FIRST

SOME OF THE MUSIC ON HIS IPOD IS DOWNLOADED FROM ITUNES, BUT MOST COMES FROM HIS FRIENDS. WHEN ONE OF THE GROUP BUYS A CD, HE OR SHE TYPICALLY MAKES COPIES FOR EVERYONE ELSE.

BEN'S READING RANGES FROM STAR WARS NOVELS TO JAPANESE MANGA, WITH A LARGE HELPING OF WEB COMICS.

BEN INSTANT MESSAGES CONSTANTLY. HE DOESN'T TEXT MUCH ON HIS CELL PHONE BUT HAS FRIENDS WHO DO.

HE PLAYS VIDEO GAMES WITH FRIENDS, MOSTLY ONLINE.

THE MAIN DIFFERENCE BETWEEN BEN'S ADOLESCENCE AND MY OWN IS SIMPLY CHOICE.

I WAS LIMITED TO WHAT WAS BROADCAST OVER THE AIRWAVES. HE'S GOT THE INTERNET. I DIDN'T HAVE TIVO (OR EVEN CABLE); HE HAS ALL THAT AND BITTORRENT, TOO.

TV SHOWS WERE MORE POPULAR IN THE SEVENTIES THAN THEY ARE NOW NOT BECAUSE THEY WERE BETTER, BUT BECAUSE WE HAD FEWER ALTERNATIVES TO COMPETE FOR OUR SCREEN ATTENTION.

THE GREAT THING ABOUT BROADCAST IS THAT IT CAN BRING ONE SHOW TO MILLIONS OF PEOPLE WITH UNMATCHABLE EFFICIENCY.

BUT IT CAN'T DO THE OPPOSITE—BRING MILLIONS OF SHOWS TO ONE PERSON. YET THAT IS EXACTLY WHAT THE INTERNET DOES SO WELL.

THE HITS NOW COMPETE WITH AN INFINITE NUMBER OF NICHE MARKETS. THE ERA OF ONE-SIZE-FITS-ALL IS ENDING, AND IN ITS PLACE IS SOMETHING NEW, A MARKET OF MULTITUDES.

THIS BOOK IS ABOUT THAT MARKET.

THAT MASS OF NICHES HAS ALWAYS EXISTED, BUT AS THE COST OF REACHING IT FALLS—CONSUMERS FINDING NICHE PRODUCTS, AND NICHE PRODUCTS FINDING CONSUMERS—IT'S SUDDENLY BECOMING A CULTURAL AND ECONOMIC FORCE TO BE RECKONED WITH.

THE NEW NICHE MARKET IS NOT REPLACING THE TRADITIONAL MARKET OF HITS, JUST SHARING THE STAGE WITH IT FOR THE FIRST TIME.

THINK OF THESE FALLING DISTRIBUTION COSTS AS A DROPPING WATERLINE OR A RECEDING TIDE.

AS THEY FALL, THEY REVEAL A NEW LAND THAT HAS BEEN THERE ALL ALONG, JUST UNDERWATER.

6

THEY ARE THE MOVIES THAT DIDN'T MAKE IT TO YOUR LOCAL THEATER, THE MUSIC NOT PLAYED ON THE LOCAL ROCK RADIO STATION, THE SPORTS EQUIPMENT NOT SOLD AT WALMART.

NOW THEY'RE AVAILABLE, VIA NETFLIX, ITUNES, AMAZON, OR JUST SOME RANDOM PLACE GOOGLE TURNED UP. THE INVISIBLE MARKET HAS TURNED VISIBLE.

UNLIMITED SELECTION IS REVEALING TRUTHS ABOUT WHAT CONSUMERS WANT AND HOW THEY WANT TO GET IT IN SERVICE AFTER SERVICE—FROM DVDS AT THE RENTAL-BY-MAIL FIRM NETFLIX TO SONGS IN THE ITUNES MUSIC STORE AND RHAPSODY.

PEOPLE ARE GOING DEEP INTO THE CATALOG, DOWN THE LONG, LONG LIST OF AVAILABLE TITLES, FAR PAST WHAT'S AVAILABLE AT MOST STORES.

AND THE MORE THEY FIND, THE MORE THEY LIKE. AS THEY WANDER FARTHER FROM THE BEATEN PATH, THEY DISCOVER THEIR TASTE IS NOT AS MAINSTREAM AS THEY THOUGHT.

IF THE TWENTIETH-CENTURY ENTERTAINMENT INDUSTRY WAS ABOUT HITS, THE TWENTY-FIRST WILL BE EQUALLY ABOUT NICHES.

THE MAIN PROBLEM (IF THAT'S THE WORD) IS THAT WE LIVE IN THE PHYSICAL WORLD, AND UNTIL RECENTLY, MOST OF OUR ENTERTAINMENT MEDIA DID, TOO.

THAT WORLD PUTS DRAMATIC LIMITATIONS ON OUR ENTERTAINMENT.

THE CURSE OF TRADITIONAL RETAIL IS THE NEED TO FIND LOCAL AUDIENCES. AN AVERAGE MOVIE THEATER WILL NOT SHOW A FILM UNLESS IT CAN ATTRACT AT LEAST 1,500 PEOPLE OVER A TWO-WEEK RUN.

AN AVERAGE RECORD STORE NEEDS TO SELL AT LEAST FOUR COPIES OF A CD PER YEAR TO MAKE IT WORTH CARRYING. AND SO ON, FOR DVD RENTAL SHOPS, VIDEO-GAME STORES, BOOKSELLERS, AND NEWSSTANDS.

IN EACH CASE, RETAILERS WILL CARRY ONLY CONTENT THAT CAN GENERATE SUFFICIENT DEMAND TO EARN ITS KEEP. HOWEVER, EACH CAN PULL FROM ONLY A LIMITED LOCAL POPULATION.

THERE IS PLENTY OF GREAT ENTERTAINMENT WITH POTENTIALLY LARGE, EVEN RAPTUROUS, NATIONAL AUDIENCES THAT CANNOT CLEAR THE LOCAL RETAILER BAR.

METAL

CLEARANCE

VIDEO GAMES
50%-75% OFF

VIDEO GAME CLEARANCE
ALL PLATFORMS
(MOSTLY PS2)

ANOTHER CONSTRAINT OF THE PHYSICAL WORLD IS PHYSICS ITSELF.

THE RADIO SPECTRUM CAN CARRY ONLY SO MANY STATIONS, AND A COAXIAL CABLE ONLY SO MANY TV CHANNELS.

FOR THE PAST CENTURY, ENTERTAINMENT HAS OFFERED AN EASY SOLUTION TO THESE CONSTRAINTS: A FOCUS ON RELEASING HITS.

AFTER ALL, HITS FILL THEATERS, FLY OFF SHELVES, AND KEEP LISTENERS AND VIEWERS FROM TOUCHING THEIR DIALS AND REMOTES.

HOWEVER, MOST OF US WANT MORE THAN JUST THE HITS.

EVERYONE'S TASTE DEPARTS FROM THE MAINSTREAM SOMEWHERE, AND THE MORE WE EXPLORE ALTERNATIVES, THE MORE WE'RE DRAWN TO THEM.

HIT-DRIVEN ECONOMICS IS A CREATION OF AN AGE IN WHICH THERE JUST WASN'T ENOUGH ROOM TO CARRY EVERYTHING FOR EVERYBODY.

THIS IS THE WORLD OF SCARCITY.

NOW, WITH ONLINE DISTRIBUTION AND RETAIL, WE ARE ENTERING A WORLD OF ABUNDANCE.

FOR A BETTER LOOK AT THE WORLD OF ABUNDANCE, LET'S RETURN TO ONLINE MUSIC RETAILER, RHAPSODY.

A SUBSCRIPTION-BASED STREAMING SERVICE, RHAPSODY CURRENTLY OFFERS MORE THAN 4 MILLION TRACKS.

FROM THE PERSPECTIVE OF A STORE LIKE WALMART, THE MUSIC INDUSTRY STOPS AT LESS THAN 60,000 TRACKS.

HOWEVER, FOR ONLINE RETAILERS LIKE RHAPSODY THE MARKET IS SEEMINGLY NEVER-ENDING. NOT ONLY IS EVERY ONE OF RHAPSODY'S TOP 60,000 TRACKS STREAMED AT LEAST ONCE EACH MONTH, BUT THE SAME IS TRUE FOR ITS TOP 600,000, TOP 900,000, AND BEYOND.

AS FAST AS RHAPSODY ADDS TRACKS TO ITS LIBRARY, THOSE SONGS FIND AN AUDIENCE, EVEN IF IT'S JUST A HANDFUL OF PEOPLE EVERY MONTH, SOMEWHERE IN THE WORLD.

THIS IS THE LONG TAIL.

YOU CAN FIND EVERYTHING OUT HERE IN THE LONG TAIL.

THERE'S THE BACK CATALOG, FOR OLDER ALBUMS STILL FONDLY REMEMBERED BY LONGTIME FANS, OR REDISCOVERED BY NEW ONES. THERE ARE LIVE TRACKS, B-SIDES, REMIXES, EVEN COVERS. THERE ARE NICHES BY THE THOUSANDS, GENRES WITHIN GENRES, WITHIN GENRES.

OH SURE, THERE'S ALSO A LOT OF CRAP HERE IN THE LONG TAIL. BUT THEN AGAIN, THERE'S AN AWFUL LOT OF CRAP HIDING BETWEEN THE RADIO TRACKS ON HIT ALBUMS, TOO.

UNLIKE THE CD—WHERE EACH CRAP TRACK COSTS PERHAPS ONE-TWELFTH OF A $15 ALBUM PRICE—ALL OF THE CRAP TRACKS ONLINE JUST SIT HARMLESSLY ON SOME SERVER, IGNORED BY A MARKETPLACE THAT EVALUATES SONGS ON THEIR OWN MERIT.

IF YOU COMBINE ENOUGH OF THE NON-HITS, YOU'VE ACTUALLY ESTABLISHED A MARKET THAT RIVALS THE HITS.

TAKE BOOKS. THE AVERAGE BARNES & NOBLE SUPERSTORE CARRIES AROUND 100,000 TITLES. YET MORE THAN A QUARTER OF AMAZON'S BOOK SALES COME FROM OUTSIDE ITS TOP 100,000 TITLES.

WHEN YOU THINK ABOUT IT, MOST SUCCESSFUL INTERNET BUSINESSES ARE CAPITALIZING ON THE LONG TAIL IN ONE WAY OR ANOTHER. THESE INFINITE-SHELF-SPACE BUSINESSES HAVE EFFECTIVELY LEARNED A LESSON IN NEW MATH.

A VERY, VERY BIG NUMBER (THE PRODUCTS IN THE TAIL) MULTIPLIED BY A RELATIVELY SMALL NUMBER (THE SALES OF EACH) IS STILL EQUAL TO A VERY, VERY BIG NUMBER. AND, AGAIN, THAT VERY, VERY BIG NUMBER IS ONLY GETTING BIGGER.

ONE WAY TO THINK OF THE DIFFERENCE BETWEEN YESTERDAY'S LIMITED CHOICE AND TODAY'S ABUNDANCE IS AS IF OUR CULTURE WERE AN OCEAN AND THE ONLY FEATURES ABOVE THE SURFACE WERE ISLANDS OF HITS.

ISLANDS ARE, OF COURSE, JUST THE TIPS OF VAST UNDERSEA MOUNTAINS.

MORE THAN 99 PERCENT OF MUSIC ALBUMS ON THE MARKET TODAY ARE NOT AVAILABLE IN WALMART.

OF THE MORE THAN 200,000 FILMS, TV SHOWS, DOCUMENTARIES AND OTHER VIDEO THAT HAVE BEEN RELEASED COMMERCIALLY, THE AVERAGE BLOCKBUSTER CARRIES JUST 3,000.

SAME FOR ANY OTHER LEADING RETAILER AND PRACTICALLY ANY OTHER COMMODITY—FROM BOOKS TO KITCHEN FITTINGS.

THE VAST MAJORITY OF PRODUCTS ARE NOT AVAILABLE AT A STORE NEAR YOU.

THE CELL PHONE.

OMG! NO SHE DIDN'T!

COMMUTERS STUCK IN TRAFFIC WERE THE SALVATION OF RADIO IN THE EIGHTIES. TODAY WE'RE STILL STUCK IN TRAFFIC, BUT NOW WE'RE CHATTING ON THE PHONE.

THE 1996 TELECOMMUNICATIONS ACT.

ADDING A THOUSAND FM STATIONS TO THE DIAL, THIS LEGISLATION INCREASED COMPETITION AND DEPRESSED THE ECONOMICS OF THE INCUMBENTS.

THE FCC'S OBSCENITY CRACKDOWN.

@#$%!

IT'S ALWAYS BEEN PART OF THE FCC'S MANDATE TO POLICE WHAT'S SAID ON THE AIRWAVES, BUT IT'S RARELY EXERCISED ITS DUTY WITH AS MUCH VIGOR AS IN THE PAST FIVE YEARS.

THE RESULT: FURTHER HOMOGENIZATION.

...NOW, MORE SMOOTH JAZZ...

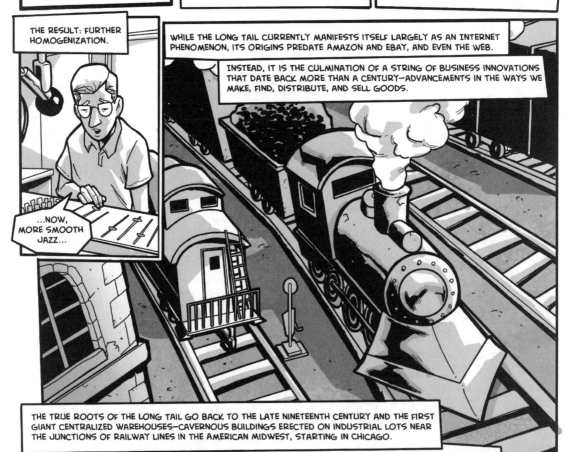

WHILE THE LONG TAIL CURRENTLY MANIFESTS ITSELF LARGELY AS AN INTERNET PHENOMENON, ITS ORIGINS PREDATE AMAZON AND EBAY, AND EVEN THE WEB.

INSTEAD, IT IS THE CULMINATION OF A STRING OF BUSINESS INNOVATIONS THAT DATE BACK MORE THAN A CENTURY—ADVANCEMENTS IN THE WAYS WE MAKE, FIND, DISTRIBUTE, AND SELL GOODS.

THE TRUE ROOTS OF THE LONG TAIL GO BACK TO THE LATE NINETEENTH CENTURY AND THE FIRST GIANT CENTRALIZED WAREHOUSES—CAVERNOUS BUILDINGS ERECTED ON INDUSTRIAL LOTS NEAR THE JUNCTIONS OF RAILWAY LINES IN THE AMERICAN MIDWEST, STARTING IN CHICAGO.

UNDER THE IMMENSE STEEL ROOFS, THE ERA OF MASSIVE CHOICE AND AVAILABILITY AROSE ON TOWERS OF WOODEN PALLETS, BUILT WITH THE BULK PURCHASING AFFORDED BY THEN-NEW MASS PRODUCTION.

THE MAN WHO FIRST SHOWED THE AMERICAN CONSUMER JUST WHAT ALL OF THIS COULD MEAN WAS RICHARD SEARS, A RAILWAY AGENT IN NORTH REDWOOD, MINNESOTA.

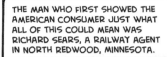

IMAGINE BEING A FARMER LIVING DEEP ON THE VAST KANSAS PRAIRIE MORE THAN A HUNDRED YEARS AGO. YOU ARE SEVERAL HOURS' RIDE FROM THE NEAREST GENERAL STORE, AND NEITHER THE STORE'S PRODUCTS NOR THE PRICE OF GASOLINE IS CHEAP.

THEN, ONE DAY, THE WEEKLY MAIL DELIVERY BRINGS YOU THE 1897 SEARS "WISH BOOK"—786 PAGES OF EVERYTHING UNDER THE SUN AT PRICES THAT CAN HARDLY BE BELIEVED.

CRAMMED INTO SOMETHING THE SIZE OF A PHONE BOOK ARE 200,000 ITEMS AND VARIATIONS, ALL DESCRIBED WITH TINY TYPE AND SOME 6,000 LITHOGRAPHIC ILLUSTRATIONS.

THE NEXT STEP IN THE MARCH TO PLENTY WAS THE SUPERSTORE.

WITH AFFORDABLE CARS AND THE ADVENT OF BETTER MODERN ROADS, SEARS' RURAL CUSTOMERS WERE NO LONGER LIMITED TO SHOPPING BY CATALOG. MEANWHILE, THE GREAT URBANIZATION OF AMERICA WAS BEGINNING, AND THOSE SAME CUSTOMERS WERE ABANDONING THE FARM FOR THE FACTORY.

CITY SHOPPERS PREFERRED STORES TO CATALOGS.

IN 1925, SEARS OPENED ONE STORE IN ITS CHICAGO MAIL-ORDER PLANT. BEFORE THE YEAR WAS OVER, SEARS HAD OPENED SEVEN MORE RETAIL STORES—FOUR IN MAIL-ORDER PLANTS. BY THE END OF 1927, IT WAS TWENTY-SEVEN STORES.

AMERICA WAS HOOKED ON CHOICE.

13

FOOD WAS THE NEXT FRONTIER.

THE FIRST SUPERMARKET WAS A KING KULLEN STORE THAT OPENED IN QUEENS, NEW YORK, ON AUGUST 4, 1930, IN THE DEPTHS OF THE GREAT DEPRESSION. THIS STORE SOLD MORE THAN ONE THOUSAND PRODUCTS, SERVING AS THE CATALYST FOR A NEW AGE IN FOOD RETAILING.

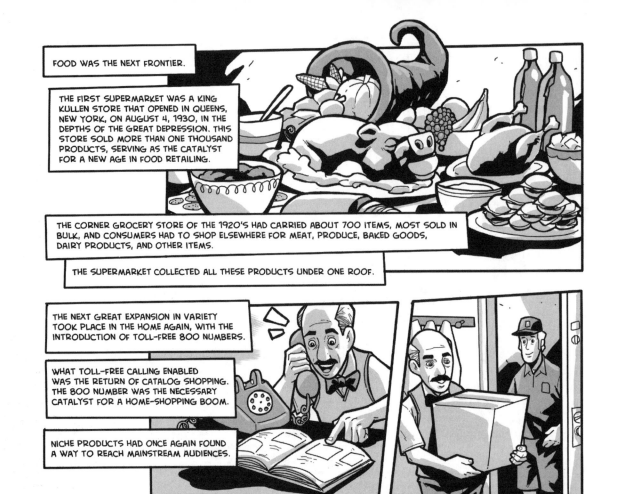

THE CORNER GROCERY STORE OF THE 1920'S HAD CARRIED ABOUT 700 ITEMS, MOST SOLD IN BULK, AND CONSUMERS HAD TO SHOP ELSEWHERE FOR MEAT, PRODUCE, BAKED GOODS, DAIRY PRODUCTS, AND OTHER ITEMS.

THE SUPERMARKET COLLECTED ALL THESE PRODUCTS UNDER ONE ROOF.

THE NEXT GREAT EXPANSION IN VARIETY TOOK PLACE IN THE HOME AGAIN, WITH THE INTRODUCTION OF TOLL-FREE 800 NUMBERS.

WHAT TOLL-FREE CALLING ENABLED WAS THE RETURN OF CATALOG SHOPPING. THE 800 NUMBER WAS THE NECESSARY CATALYST FOR A HOME-SHOPPING BOOM.

NICHE PRODUCTS HAD ONCE AGAIN FOUND A WAY TO REACH MAINSTREAM AUDIENCES.

SPORTING GOODS, BRANDED APPAREL, INTERIOR DESIGN, LINGERIE, OUTDOOR FURNITURE, HOBBIES— ALL IT TOOK WAS A PHONE CALL AND A CREDIT CARD, AND CONSUMERS WOULD HAVE THEIR PRODUCTS IN HAND IN A WEEK OR TWO.

BUT AS IMPRESSIVE AS THIS POSTAL CORNUCOPIA MIGHT HAVE SEEMED, WHAT THE PERSONAL COMPUTER COULD OFFER WOULD SOON DWARF IT.

CHECKOUT

THE RISE OF E-COMMERCE ON THE WEB IN THE EARLY 1990'S STARTED BY SIMPLY BUILDING ON THE CATALOG MODEL WITH EVEN MORE CONVENIENT ORDERING, LARGER SELECTIONS, AND BROADER REACH AT LOWER COST.

THE INTERNET PROVIDED A WAY OF OFFERING A CATALOG TO EVERYONE— WITH NO PRINTING AND NO MAILING REQUIRED. IT WOULD CLEARLY WORK EVERYWHERE CATALOGS WORKED, AND THEN SOME.

TODAY ONLINE SHOPPING HAS PASSED CATALOG SHOPPING AND NOW ACCOUNTS FOR ABOUT 5 PERCENT OF AMERICAN RETAIL SPENDING.

IT'S STILL GROWING AT A WHOPPING 25 PERCENT A YEAR.

FROM PURELY VIRTUAL RETAILERS SUCH AS EBAY TO THE ONLINE SIDE OF TRADITIONAL RETAILING, THE VIRTUES OF UNLIMITED SHELF SPACE ARE COMPELLING—ABUNDANT INFORMATION AND SMART WAYS TO FIND WHAT YOU WANT.

AS A RESULT, THERE ARE NOW LONG TAIL MARKETS PRACTICALLY EVERYWHERE YOU LOOK.

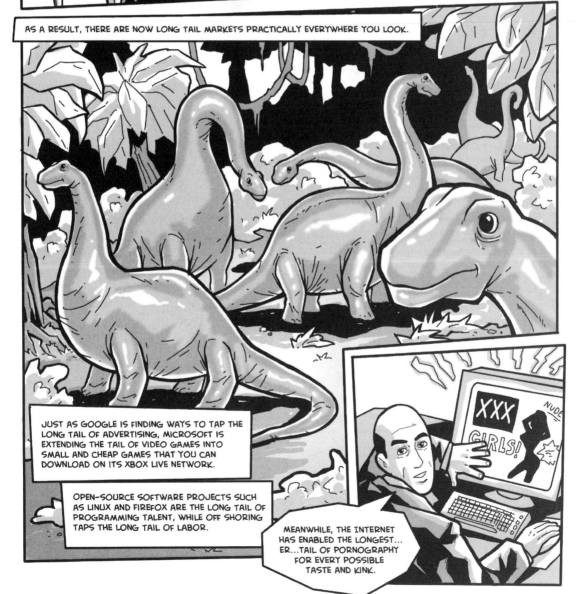

JUST AS GOOGLE IS FINDING WAYS TO TAP THE LONG TAIL OF ADVERTISING, MICROSOFT IS EXTENDING THE TAIL OF VIDEO GAMES INTO SMALL AND CHEAP GAMES THAT YOU CAN DOWNLOAD ON ITS XBOX LIVE NETWORK.

OPEN-SOURCE SOFTWARE PROJECTS SUCH AS LINUX AND FIREFOX ARE THE LONG TAIL OF PROGRAMMING TALENT, WHILE OFF SHORING TAPS THE LONG TAIL OF LABOR.

MEANWHILE, THE INTERNET HAS ENABLED THE LONGEST... ER...TAIL OF PORNOGRAPHY FOR EVERY POSSIBLE TASTE AND KINK.

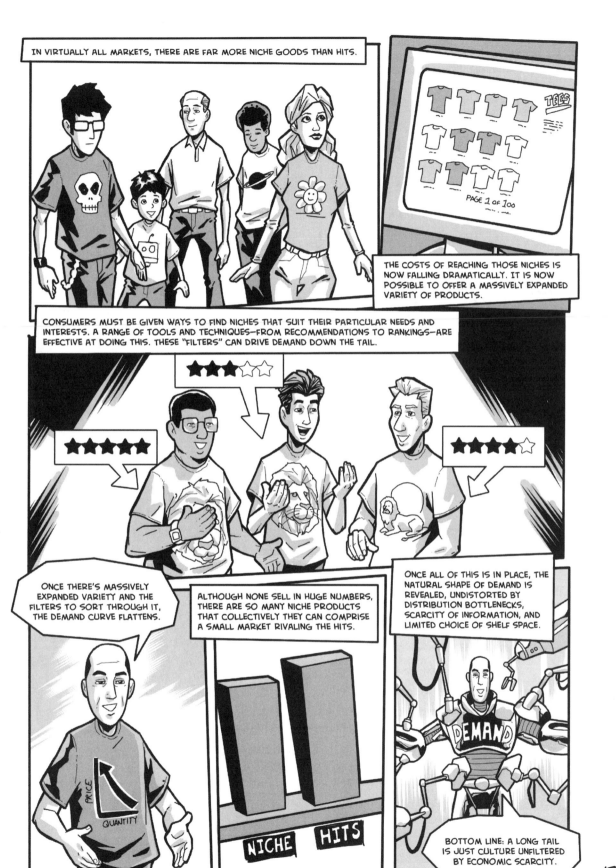

IN VIRTUALLY ALL MARKETS, THERE ARE FAR MORE NICHE GOODS THAN HITS.

TEES

PAGE 1 OF 100

THE COSTS OF REACHING THOSE NICHES IS NOW FALLING DRAMATICALLY. IT IS NOW POSSIBLE TO OFFER A MASSIVELY EXPANDED VARIETY OF PRODUCTS.

CONSUMERS MUST BE GIVEN WAYS TO FIND NICHES THAT SUIT THEIR PARTICULAR NEEDS AND INTERESTS. A RANGE OF TOOLS AND TECHNIQUES—FROM RECOMMENDATIONS TO RANKINGS—ARE EFFECTIVE AT DOING THIS. THESE "FILTERS" CAN DRIVE DEMAND DOWN THE TAIL.

ONCE THERE'S MASSIVELY EXPANDED VARIETY AND THE FILTERS TO SORT THROUGH IT, THE DEMAND CURVE FLATTENS.

PRICE
QUANTITY

ALTHOUGH NONE SELL IN HUGE NUMBERS, THERE ARE SO MANY NICHE PRODUCTS THAT COLLECTIVELY THEY CAN COMPRISE A SMALL MARKET RIVALING THE HITS.

NICHE   HITS

ONCE ALL OF THIS IS IN PLACE, THE NATURAL SHAPE OF DEMAND IS REVEALED, UNDISTORTED BY DISTRIBUTION BOTTLENECKS, SCARCITY OF INFORMATION, AND LIMITED CHOICE OF SHELF SPACE.

DEMAND

BOTTOM LINE: A LONG TAIL IS JUST CULTURE UNFILTERED BY ECONOMIC SCARCITY.

NONE OF THE AFOREMENTIONED HAPPENS WITHOUT ONE BIG ECONOMIC TRIGGER: REDUCING THE COSTS OF REACHING NICHES.

THE FIRST FORCE IS DEMOCRATIZING THE TOOLS OF PRODUCTION.

THE BEST EXAMPLE OF THIS IS THE PERSONAL COMPUTER, WHICH HAS PUT EVERYTHING FROM THE PRINTING PRESS TO FILM AND MUSIC STUDIOS IN THE HANDS OF ANYONE.

MUSIC STUDIO

WHAT CAUSES THOSE COSTS TO FALL? ALTHOUGH THE ANSWER VARIES FROM MARKET TO MARKET, THE EXPLANATION USUALLY INVOLVES ONE OR MORE OF THREE POWERFUL FORCES COMING INTO PLAY.

THE SECOND FORCE IS CUTTING THE COSTS OF CONSUMPTION BY DEMOCRATIZING DISTRIBUTION.

THE PC MADE EVERYONE A PRODUCER OR PUBLISHER, BUT IT WAS THE INTERNET THAT MADE EVERYONE A DISTRIBUTOR.

TRACK UPLOADING
73% COMPLETE

THE THIRD FORCE IS CONNECTING SUPPLY AND DEMAND, INTRODUCING CONSUMERS TO THESE NEW AND NEWLY AVAILABLE GOODS AND DRIVING DEMAND DOWN THE TAIL.

THIS CAN TAKE THE FORM OF ANYTHING FROM GOOGLE'S WISDOM-OF-CROWDS SEARCH TO ITUNES' RECOMMENDATIONS, ALONG WITH WORD-OF-MOUTH, FROM BLOG TO CUSTOMER REVIEWS.

BASED ON YOUR PURCHASE HISTORY, WE RECOMMEND THIS PRODUCT ALSO!

THINK OF EACH OF THESE FORCES AS REPRESENTING A NEW SET OF OPPORTUNITIES IN THE EMERGING LONG TAIL MARKETPLACE.

THE DEMOCRATIZED TOOLS OF PRODUCTION ARE LEADING TO A HUGE INCREASE IN THE NUMBERS OF PRODUCERS.

HYPEREFFICIENT DIGITAL ECONOMICS ARE LEADING TO NEW MARKETS AND MARKETPLACES.

AND FINALLY, THE ABILITY TO TAP THE DISTRIBUTED INTELLIGENCE OF MILLIONS OF CONSUMERS TO MATCH PEOPLE WITH THE STUFF THAT SUITS THEM BEST IS LEADING TO THE RISE OF ALL SORTS OF NEW RECOMMENDATION AND MARKETING METHODS, ESSENTIALLY SERVING AS THE NEW TASTEMAKERS.

JUST AS THE ELECTRIC GUITAR AND THE GARAGE DEMOCRATIZED POP MUSIC FORTY YEARS AGO, DESKTOP CREATION AND PRODUCTION TOOLS ARE DEMOCRITIZING THE STUDIO.

DIGITAL VIDEO CAMERAS AND DESKTOP EDITING SUITES ARE PUTTING THE SORT OF TOOLS INTO THE HANDS OF THE AVERAGE HOME MOVIEMAKER THAT WERE ONCE RESERVED FOR THE PROFESSIONALS ALONE.

I NEED MORE "GRRR"!

THEN THERE'S THE WRITTEN WORD, ALWAYS THE LEADING EDGE OF EGALITARIANISM.

MOVIE REVIEW BLOG

I LOVED IT!

ALTHOUGH IT WAS THE PHOTOCOPIER THAT FIRST PUT LIE TO THE APHORISM THAT "THE POWER OF THE PRESS GOES TO THOSE WHO OWN THEM," IT'S BLOGGING THAT HAS REALLY SPARKED THE RENAISSANCE OF THE AMATEUR PUBLISHER.

TODAY, MILLIONS OF PEOPLE PUBLISH DAILY FOR AN AUDIENCE THAT IS COLLECTIVELY LARGER THAN ANY SINGLE MAINSTREAM MEDIA OUTLET CAN CLAIM.

WHAT SPARKED BLOGGING WAS DEMOCRATIZED TOOLS: THE ARRIVAL OF SIMPLE, CHEAP SOFTWARE AND SERVICES THAT MADE PUBLISHING ONLINE SO EASY THAT ANYONE CAN DO IT.

SO, TOO, FOR DESKTOP PHOTO EDITING AND PRINTING, VIDEO GAMES THAT ENCOURAGE PLAYERS TO CREATE AND SHARE THEIR OWN ALTERNATIVE LEVELS, AND PRINT-ON-DEMAND BOOK PUBLISHING.

A FEW DECADES AGO, THERE WERE TWO REASONS WHY MOST OF US WEREN'T MAKING HIT MOVIES...WE DIDN'T HAVE ACCESS TO THE NECESSARY TOOLS... AND WE DIDN'T HAVE THE TALENT.

TODAY, THERE'S ONLY ONE EXCUSE—AND EVEN THAT IS NOT AS SOLID AS IT WAS.

HOLLYWOOD, FOR ALL ITS EFFICIENCIES, CAN'T FIND EVERY POTENTIALLY GREAT FILMMAKER ON THE PLANET. TECHNOLOGY, CHEAP AND UBIQUITOUS, CAN DO FAR BETTER. ONCE UPON A TIME, TALENT EVENTUALLY MADE ITS WAY TO THE TOOLS OF PRODUCTION: NOW IT'S THE OTHER WAY AROUND.

THE CONSEQUENCE OF ALL THIS IS THAT WE'RE STARTING TO SHIFT FROM BEING PASSIVE CONSUMERS TO ACTIVE PRODUCERS.

AND WE'RE DOING IT FOR THE LOVE OF IT (THE WORD "AMATEUR" DERIVES FROM THE LATIN AMATOR, "LOVER", FROM AMARE, "TO LOVE").

TODAY, MILLIONS OF ORDINARY PEOPLE HAVE THE TOOLS AND THE ROLE MODELS TO BECOME AMATEUR PRODUCERS.

SOME OF THEM WILL ALSO HAVE TALENT AND VISION. BECAUSE THE MEANS OF PRODUCTION HAVE SPREAD SO WIDELY AND TO SO MANY PEOPLE, THE TALENTED AND VISIONARY ONES, EVEN IF THEY'RE JUST A SMALL FRACTION OF THE TOTAL, ARE BECOMING A FORCE TO BE RECKONED WITH.

THE EFFECT OF THIS SHIFT MEANS THAT THE LONG TAIL WILL BE POPULATED AT A PACE NEVER BEFORE SEEN.

WIKIPEDIA, FOR EXAMPLE, OFFERS MORE THAN 2 MILLION ARTICLES IN ENGLISH—COMPARED WITH BRITANNICA'S 120,000 (65,000 IN THE PRINT EDITION) AND ENCARTA'S 60,000—FASHIONED BY MORE THAN 75,000 CONTRIBUTORS.

ALL YOU NEED TO CONTRIBUTE TO WIKIPEDIA IS INTERNET ACCESS: EVERY ENTRY HAS AN "EDIT THIS PAGE" BUTTON ON IT.

THE BEAUTY OF WIKIPEDIA IS THAT THERE IS PRACTICALLY NO SUBJECT SO NARROW THAT IT CAN'T HAVE AN ENTRY.

AS A WHOLE, WIKIPEDIA IS ARGUABLY THE BEST ENCYCLOPEDIA IN THE WORLD: BIGGER, MORE UP-TO-DATE, AND IN MANY CASES DEEPER THAN EVEN BRITANNICA.

BUT AT THE INDIVIDUAL ENTRY LEVEL, THE QUALITY VARIES.

ALONG WITH ARTICLES OF BREATHTAKING SCHOLARSHIP AND ERUDITION, THERE ARE PLENTY OF "STUBS" (PLACEHOLDER ENTRIES) AND EVEN AUTOGENERATED SPAM.

THE POINT IS NOT THAT EVERY WIKIPEDIA ENTRY IS PROBABILISTIC, BUT THAT THE ENTIRE ENCYCLOPEDIA BEHAVES PROBABILISTICALLY.

YOUR ODDS OF GETTING A SUBSTANTIVE, UP-TO-DATE, AND ACCURATE ENTRY FOR ANY GIVEN SUBJECT ARE EXCELLENT ON WIKIPEDIA, EVEN IF EVERY INDIVIDUAL ENTRY ISN'T EXCELLENT.

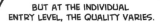

WHAT MAKES WIKIPEDIA REALLY EXTRAORDINARY IS THAT IT IMPROVES OVER TIME, ORGANICALLY HEALING ITSELF AS IF ITS HUGE AND GROWING ARMY OF USERS WERE AN IMMUNE SYSTEM, EVER VIGILANT AND QUICK TO RESPOND TO ANYTHING THAT THREATENS THE ORGANISM.

THE TRADITIONAL PROCESS OF CREATING AN ENCYCLOPEDIA—PROFESSIONAL EDITORS, ACADEMIC WRITERS, AND PEER REVIEW— AIMS FOR PERFECTION.

IT SELDOM GETS THERE, BUT THE PURSUIT OF ACCURACY AND CLARITY RESULTS IN A WORK THAT IS CONSISTENT AND RELIABLE, BUT ALSO INCREDIBLY TIME-CONSUMING AND EXPENSIVE TO PRODUCE.

LIKEWISE FOR MOST OTHER PRODUCTS OF THE PROFESSIONAL PUBLISHING INDUSTRY:

ONE CAN EXPECT THAT A BOOK WILL, IN FACT, HAVE PRINTING ON BOTH SIDES OF THE PAGES WHERE INTENDED AND WILL BE MORE OR LESS SPELLED CORRECTLY. THERE IS A QUALITY THRESHOLD, BELOW WHICH THE WORK DOES NOT FALL.

WITH PROBABILISTIC SYSTEMS, THOUGH, THERE IS ONLY A STATISTICAL LEVEL OF QUALITY, WHICH IS TO SAY: SOME THINGS WILL BE GREAT, SOME THINGS WILL BE MEDIOCRE, AND SOME THINGS WILL BE ABSOLUTELY CRAPPY.

THE MISTAKE OF MANY OF THE CRITICS IS TO EXPECT OTHERWISE. WIKIPEDIA IS SIMPLY A DIFFERENT ANIMAL FROM BRITANNICA. IT'S A LIVING COMMUNITY RATHER THAN A STATIC REFERENCE WORK.

GOOD

MEDIOCRE

CRAPPY

QUALITY OF THINGS

THE RESULT IS A VERY DIFFERENT KIND OF ENCYCLOPEDIA, ONE COMPLETELY UNBOUNDED BY SPACE AND PRODUCTION CONSTRAINTS.

IT OFFERS ALL THE EXPECTED ENTRIES OF ANY WORLD-CLASS REFERENCE WORK AND THEN HUNDREDS OF THOUSANDS OF UNEXPECTED ONES, RANGING FROM QUANTUM MECHANICS TO BIOGRAPHICAL ENTRIES ON COMIC BOOK CHARACTERS.

THIS IS THE WORLD OF "PEER PRODUCTION," THE EXTRAORDINARY INTERNET-ENABLED PHENOMENON OF MASS VOLUNTEERISM AND AMATEURISM.

WE ARE AT THE DAWN OF AN AGE WHERE MOST PRODUCERS IN ANY DOMAIN ARE UNPAID, AND THE MAIN DIFFERENCE BETWEEN THEM AND THEIR PROFESSIONAL COUNTERPARTS IS SIMPLY THE (SHRINKING) GAP IN THE RESOURCES AVAILABLE TO THEM TO EXTEND THE AMBITION OF THEIR WORK.

WHEN THE TOOLS OF PRODUCTION ARE AVAILABLE TO EVERYONE, EVERYONE BECOMES A PRODUCER.

WHY DO THEY DO IT? WHY DOES ANYONE CREATE SOMETHING OF VALUE WITHOUT A BUSINESS PLAN OR EVEN THE PROSPECT OF A PAYCHECK?

THE QUESTION IS A KEY ONE TO UNDERSTANDING THE LONG TAIL, PARTLY BECAUSE SO MUCH OF WHAT POPULATES THE CURVES DOES NOT START WITH COMMERCIAL AIM.

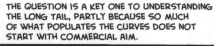

THIS QUESTION MATTERS BECAUSE IT REPRESENTS YET ANOTHER EXAMPLE OF WHERE OUR PRESUMPTIONS ABOUT MARKETS MUST BE RETHOUGHT. THE MOTIVES TO CREATE ARE NOT THE SAME IN THE HEAD AS THEY ARE ON THE TAIL.

UP AT THE HEAD, WHERE PRODUCTS BENEFIT FROM THE POWERFUL, BUT EXPENSIVE, CHANNELS OF MASS-MARKET DISTRIBUTION, BUSINESS CONSIDERATIONS RULE.

IT'S THE DOMAIN OF PROFESSIONALS AND AS MUCH AS THEY MIGHT LOVE WHAT THEY DO, IT'S A JOB, TOO. THE COSTS OF PRODUCTION AND DISTRIBUTION ARE TOO HIGH TO LET ECONOMICS TAKE A BACKSEAT TO CREATIVITY. MONEY DRIVES THE PROCESS.

DOWN IN THE TAIL, WHERE DISTRIBUTION AND PRODUCTION COSTS ARE LOW, BUSINESS CONSIDERATIONS ARE OFTEN SECONDARY.

INSTEAD, PEOPLE CREATE FOR A VARIETY OF OTHER REASONS—EXPRESSION, FUN, EXPERIMENTATION, AND SO ON. THE REASON ONE MIGHT CALL IT AN ECONOMY AT ALL IS THAT THERE IS A COIN OF THE REALM THAT CAN BE EVERY BIT AS MOTIVATING AS MONEY: REPUTATION.

THERE ARE PLENTY OF OTHER ARTISTS AND PRODUCERS WHO SEE FREE PEER-TO-PEER DISTRIBUTION AS LOW-COST MARKETING.

MUSICIANS CAN TURN THAT INTO AN AUDIENCE FOR THEIR LIVE SHOWS, INDIE FILMMAKERS TREAT IT AS A VIRAL RESUME, AND ACADEMICS TREAT FREE DOWNLOADS OF THEIR PAPERS AS A WAY TO INCREASE THEIR IMPACT AND AUDIENCE.

THE LONG TAILS

WE THINK OF BOOKS THROUGH A COMMERCIAL LENS, ASSUMING THAT MOST AUTHORS WANT TO WRITE A BEST-SELLER AND GET RICH.

BUT THE REALITY IS THAT THE VAST MAJORITY OF AUTHORS NOT ONLY WON'T BECOME BEST-SELLERS, BUT ALSO AREN'T EVEN TRYING TO WRITE A HUGELY POPULAR BOOK.

MY FAMILY RECIPES

FROM FILMMAKERS TO BLOGGERS, PRODUCERS OF ALL SORTS THAT START IN THE TAIL WITH FEW EXPECTATIONS OF COMMERCIAL SUCCESS CAN AFFORD TO TAKE CHANCES.

THEY'RE WILLING TO TAKE MORE RISKS, BECAUSE THEY HAVE LESS TO LOSE. THERE'S NO NEED FOR PERMISSION, A BUSINESS PLAN, OR EVEN CAPITAL.

THE QUEST FOR MASS-MARKET ACCEPTANCE REQUIRED COMPROMISE—A WILLINGNESS TO PICK TOPICS OF BROAD RATHER THAN NARROW INTEREST, AND TO WRITE IN CONVERSATIONAL RATHER THAN ACADEMIC STYLE.

MOST WRITERS CAN'T DO THAT AND MANY OTHERS WON'T. INSTEAD, THE VAST MAJORITY OF AUTHORS CHOOSE TO FOLLOW THEIR PASSIONS AND ASSUME THEY WON'T MAKE MONEY. MANY WANT NO MORE THAN TO BE READ BY SOME GROUP THAT MATTERS TO THEM—FROM THEIR PEERS TO LIKE-MINDED SOULS.

LEMONADE

25¢

THE TOOLS OF CREATIVITY ARE CHEAP, AND TALENT IS MORE WIDELY DISTRIBUTED THAN WE KNOW.

SEEN THIS WAY, THE LONG TAIL PROMISED TO BECOME THE CRUCIBLE OF CREATIVITY, A PLACE WHERE IDEAS FORM AND GROW BEFORE EVOLVING INTO COMMERCIAL FORM.

THE LOWER THE COSTS OF SELLING, THE MORE YOU CAN SELL.

AS SUCH, AGGREGATORS ARE A MANIFESTATION OF THE SECOND FORCE, DEMOCRATIZING DISTRIBUTION. THEY ALL LOWER THE BARRIER TO MARKET ENTRY, ALLOWING MORE AND MORE THINGS TO CROSS THAT BAR AND GET OUT THERE TO FIND THEIR AUDIENCE.

THERE ARE LITERALLY THOUSANDS OF EXAMPLES, BUT I'LL GIVE JUST A FEW HERE.

GOOGLE AGGREGATES THE LONG TAIL OF ADVERTISING.

EAT AT JOES

EAT AT JOES

EAT AT JOES

EAT AT JOES

RHAPSODY AND ITUNES AGGREGATE THE LONG TAIL OF MUSIC.

NETFLIX DOES THE SAME FOR THE LONG TAIL OF MOVIES.

EBAY AGGREGATES THE LONG TAIL OF PHYSICAL GOODS AND THE LONG TAIL OF MERCHANTS WHO SELL THEM.

I'LL FOCUS ON THE BUSINESS AGGREGATORS.

THEY FALL MOSTLY INTO FIVE CATEGORIES.

☐ PHYSICAL GOODS
☐ DIGITAL GOODS
☐ ADVERTISING/SERVICES
☐ INFORMATION
☐ COMMUNITIES/USER-CREATED CONTENT.

LET'S START BY CONTRASTING THE FIRST CATEGORY OF ONLINE AGGREGATOR BUSINESSES, SELLING PHYSICAL GOODS ONLINE, WITH THE SECOND, SELLING DIGITAL GOODS ONLINE.

DOWNLOAD

THEY'RE BOTH LONG TAIL OPPORTUNITIES, BUT THE SECOND ONE CAN EXTEND FARTHER DOWN THE TAIL THAN THE FIRST.

THE ONLINE RETAILERS OF PHYSICAL GOODS, CAN OFFER INVENTORY HUNDREDS OF TIMES GREATER THAN THEIR BRICKS-AND-MORTAR COUNTERPARTS, BUT EVENTUALLY EVEN THEY HIT A LIMIT.

BY CONTRAST, THE COMPANIES THAT SELL DIGITAL GOODS, FROM ALBUMS OR SONGS ON ITUNES TO TV SHOWS OR AMATEUR CLIPS ON GOOGLE VIDEO, CAN THEORETICALLY GO ALL THE WAY DOWN THE TAIL, EXPANDING THE VARIETY THEY OFFER TO ENCOMPASS EVERYTHING AVAILABLE.

WE CALL THE FIRST TYPE A HYBRID RETAILER BECAUSE IT'S A CROSS BETWEEN THE ECONOMICS OF MAIL ORDER (PHYSICAL) AND THE INTERNET (DIGITAL).

THE ONLY WAY TO REACH ALL THE WAY DOWN THE TAIL—FROM THE BIGGEST HITS DOWN TO ALL THE GARAGE BANDS OF PAST AND PRESENT—IS TO ABANDON ATOMS ENTIRELY AND BASE ALL TRANSACTIONS, FROM BEGINNING TO END, IN THE WORLD OF BITS.

THAT'S THE STRUCTURE OF THE SECOND CLASS OF AGGREGATOR, THE PURE DIGITAL RETAILER.

WITH THE PURE DIGITAL MODEL, EACH PRODUCT IS SIMPLY A DATABASE ENTRY, COSTING EFFECTIVELY NOTHING.

THE DISTRIBUTION COSTS ARE SIMPLY BROADBAND MEGABYTES, BOUGHT IN BULK AT FASTDROPPING COSTS INCURRED ONLY WHEN THE PRODUCT IS ORDERED. WHAT'S MORE, PURE DIGITAL RETAILERS CAN CHOOSE BETWEEN SELLING GOODS AS STAND-ALONE PRODUCTS OR AS A SERVICE.

THE ULTIMATE COST REDUCTION IS ELIMINATING ATOMS ENTIRELY AND DEALING ONLY IN BITS.

PURE DIGITAL AGGREGATORS STORE THEIR INVENTORY ON HARD DRIVES AND DELIVER IT VIA BROADBAND PIPES. THE MARGINAL COST OF MANUFACTURING, SHELVING, AND DISTRIBUTION IS CLOSE TO ZERO, AND ROYALTIES ARE PAID ONLY WHEN THE GOODS ARE SOLD. IT'S THE ULTIMATE ON-DEMAND MARKET.

THE OVERWHELMING TREND OF OUR AGE IS TO TAKE PRODUCTS THAT WERE ONCE DELIVERED AS PHYSICAL GOODS, FIND WAYS TO TURN THEM INTO DATA, AND STREAM THEM INTO YOUR HOME...

GRIND·O·MATIC

...FROM COMMERCIAL VIDEO-ON-DEMAND SERVICES PROVIDED BY CABLE COMPANIES TO WEB-BASED VIDEO AGGREGATORS SUCH AS GOOGLE VIDEO.

VIDEO GAMES ARE NOW INCREASINGLY STREAMED AS BITS TO GAME CONSOLES IN THE LIVING ROOM.

AND SO, TOO, FOR EBOOKS AND AUDIO BOOKS, ONLINE NEWSPAPERS, AND MAGAZINES, MOVIES, AND SOFTWARE.

ALL WERE ONCE DELIVERED ON PAPER OR PLASTIC, NECESSITATING ALL THE COMPLEXITIES OF PHYSICAL INVENTORY AND DELIVERY. ALL ARE NOW JOINED BY DIGITAL VERSION, WITH CORRESPONDING DIGITAL ECONOMICS.

THE EXPERIENCE IS NOT ALWAYS THE SAME, WHICH IS WHY PAPER BOOKS AND MAGAZINES ARE STILL THE PREFERRED VERSION FOR MANY. BUT THE FUNCTIONAL GAP IS SHRINKING. AND THE DISTRIBUTION ADVANTAGES OF THE DIGITAL VERSIONS ARE IRRESISTIBLE.

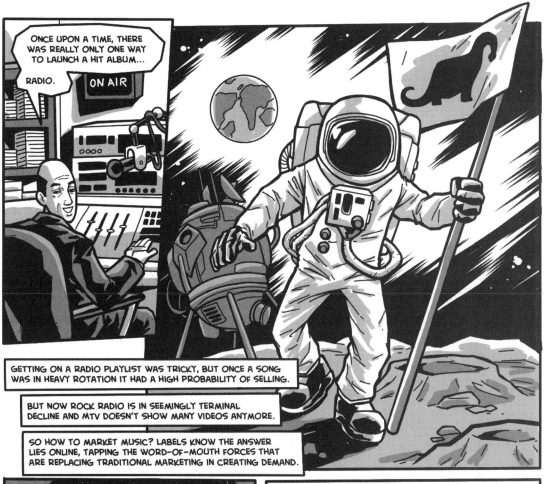

ONCE UPON A TIME, THERE WAS REALLY ONLY ONE WAY TO LAUNCH A HIT ALBUM...

RADIO.

ON AIR

GETTING ON A RADIO PLAYLIST WAS TRICKY, BUT ONCE A SONG WAS IN HEAVY ROTATION IT HAD A HIGH PROBABILITY OF SELLING.

BUT NOW ROCK RADIO IS IN SEEMINGLY TERMINAL DECLINE AND MTV DOESN'T SHOW MANY VIDEOS ANYMORE.

SO HOW TO MARKET MUSIC? LABELS KNOW THE ANSWER LIES ONLINE, TAPPING THE WORD-OF-MOUTH FORCES THAT ARE REPLACING TRADITIONAL MARKETING IN CREATING DEMAND.

WE'RE ENTERING AN ERA OF RADICAL CHANGE FOR MARKETERS.

FAITH IN ADVERTISING AND THE INSTITUTIONS THAT PAY FOR IT IS WANING, WHILE FAITH IN INDIVIDUALS IS ON THE RISE. TOP-DOWN MESSAGING IS LOSING TRACTION, WHILE BOTTOM-UP BUZZ IS GAINING POWER.

THE NEW TASTEMAKERS ARE US. WORD-OF-MOUTH IS NOW A PUBLIC CONVERSATION, CARRIED IN BLOG COMMENTS AND CUSTOMER REVIEWS, EXHAUSTIVELY COLLATED AND MEASURED.

THE ANTS HAVE MEGAPHONES.

YAHOO! MUSIC RATINGS, GOOGLE PAGERANK, FACEBOOK FRIENDS, NETFLIX USER-REVIEWS – THESE ARE ALL MANIFESTATIONS OF THE WISDOM OF THE CROWD.

MILLIONS OF REGULAR PEOPLE ARE THE NEW TASTEMAKERS.

SOME OF THEM ACT AS INDIVIDUALS, OTHERS ARE PARTS OF GROUPS ORGANIZED AROUND SHARED INTERESTS, AND STILL OTHERS ARE SIMPLY HERDS OF CONSUMERS AUTOMATICALLY TRACKED BY SOFTWARE WATCHING THEIR EVERY BEHAVIOR.

AMPLIFIED WORD OF MOUTH IS THE MANIFESTATION OF THE THIRD FORCE OF THE LONG TAIL: TAPPING CONSUMER SENTIMENT TO CONNECT SUPPLY TO DEMAND.

THE NEW TASTEMAKERS ARE SIMPLY PEOPLE WHOSE OPINIONS ARE RESPECTED. THEY INFLUENCE BEHAVIOR, OFTEN ENCOURAGING OTHERS TO TRY THINGS THEY WOULDN'T OTHERWISE PURSUE. SOME OF THESE NEW TASTEMAKERS ARE THE TRADITIONAL PROFESSIONALS: MOVIE AND MUSIC CRITICS, EDITORS, OR PRODUCT TESTERS.

OTHER TASTEMAKERS ARE CELEBRITIES, WHO ARE ANOTHER SORT OF TRUSTED GUIDE, AND WHOSE INFLUENCE ON CONSUMPTION CONTINUES TO GROW.

BUT NOT ALL CELEBRITIES ARE HOLLYWOOD STARS. AS OUR CULTURE FRAGMENTS INTO A MILLION TINY MICROCULTURES, WE ARE EXPERIENCING A CORRESPONDING RISE OF MICROCELEBRITIES.

THE CATCH-ALL PHRASE FOR RECOMMENDATIONS AND ALL THE OTHER TOOLS THAT HELP YOU FIND QUALITY IN THE LONG TAIL IS FILTERS.

THESE TECHNOLOGIES AND SERVICES SIFT THROUGH A VAST ARRAY OF CHOICES TO PRESENT YOU WITH THE ONES THAT ARE MOST RIGHT FOR YOU.

IN TODAY'S LONG TAIL MARKETS, THE MAIN EFFECT OF FILTERS IS TO HELP PEOPLE MOVE FROM THE WORLD THEY KNOW ("HITS") TO THE WORLD THEY DON'T ("NICHES") VIA A ROUTE THAT IS BOTH, COMFORTABLE AND TAILORED TO THEIR TASTES.

IN A SENSE, GOOD FILTERS HAVE THE EFFECT OF DRIVING DEMAND DOWN THE TAIL BY REVEALING GOODS AND SERVICES THAT APPEAL MORE THAN THE LOWEST-COMMON-DENOMINATOR FARE THAT CROWDS THE NARROW CHANNELS OF TRADITIONAL MASS-MARKET DISTRIBUTION.

NOT LONG AGO, THERE WERE FAR FEWER WAYS TO FIND NEW MUSIC. ASIDE FROM PERSONAL RECOMMENDATIONS, THERE WERE EDITORIAL REVIEWS IN MAGAZINES, PERHAPS THE ADVICE OF A WELL-INFORMED RECORD STORE CLERK, AND THE BIGGEST OF THEM ALL, RADIO AIRPLAY.

RADIO PLAYLISTS, ESPECIALLY TODAY, ARE THE PRIME EXAMPLE OF THE BEST-KNOWN FILTER OF ALL, THE POPULARITY LIST.

BUT IN A LONG TAIL WORLD, WITH SO MANY OTHER FILTERS AVAILABLE, THE WEAKNESSES OF TOP 10 LISTS ARE BECOMING MORE AND MORE CLEAR.

THERE'S NOTHING WRONG WITH RANKING BY POPULARITY—AFTER ALL, THAT'S JUST ANOTHER EXAMPLE OF A "WISDOM OF CROWDS" FILTER—BUT ALL TOO OFTEN THESE LISTS LUMP TOGETHER ALL SORTS OF NICHES, GENRES, SUBGENRES, AND CATEGORIES INTO ONE UNHOLY MESS.

THESE LISTS ARE, IN OTHER WORDS, A SEMI-RANDOM COLLECTION OF TOTALLY DISPARATE THINGS.

TO USE AN ANALOGY, TOP-BLOG LISTS ARE AKIN TO RANKING THE BEST-SELLERS IN THE SUPERMARKET.

THIS IS POINTLESS. NOBODY CARES IF BANANAS OUTSELL SOFT DRINKS. WHAT THEY CARE ABOUT IS WHICH SOFT DRINK OUTSELLS WHICH OTHER SOFT DRINK. LISTS MAKE SENSE ONLY IN CONTEXT, COMPARING LIKE WITH LIKE WITHIN A CATEGORY.

1. MILK
2. MIXED GRAIN BREAD
3. BANANAS
4. CRUNCHIOS CEREAL
5. DIET WHOOP... ODA

THIS IS ANOTHER REMINDER THAT YOU HAVE TO TREAT NICHES AS NICHES. WHEN YOU LOOK AT A WIDELY DIVERSE THREE-DIMENSIONAL MARKET PLACE THROUGH A ONE-DIMENSIONAL LENS, YOU GET NONSENSE. IT'S A LIST, BUT IT'S A LIST WITHOUT MEANING.

WHAT MATTERS IS THE RANKINGS WITHIN A GENRE, NOT ACROSS GENRES.

WHY ARE FILTERS SO IMPORTANT TO A FUNCTIONING LONG TAIL? BECAUSE WITHOUT THEM, THE LONG TAIL RISKS JUST BEING NOISE.

THE JOB OF FILTERS IS TO SCREEN OUT THAT NOISE. CALL IT PULLING WHEAT FROM CHAFF OR DIAMONDS FROM THE ROUGH, THE ROLE OF A FILTER IS TO ELEVATE THE FEW PRODUCTS THAT ARE RIGHT FOR WHOEVER IS LOOKING AND SUPPRESS THE MANY THAT AREN'T.

IN A LONG TAIL MARKET, WHICH INCLUDES NEARLY EVERYTHING, NOISE CAN BE A HUGE PROBLEM. INDEED, IF LEFT UNCHECKED, NOISE—RANDOM CONTENT OR PRODUCTS OF POOR QUALITY—CAN KILL A MARKET.

ONE OF THE MOST FREQUENT MISTAKES PEOPLE MAKE ABOUT THE LONG TAIL IS TO ASSUME THAT THINGS THAT DON'T SELL WELL ARE "NOT AS GOOD" AS THINGS THAT DO SELL WELL. OR, TO PUT IT ANOTHER WAY, THEY ASSUME THAT THE LONG TAIL IS FULL OF CRAP.

FIRST, LET'S GET ONE THING STRAIGHT. THE LONG TAIL IS INDEED FULL OF CRAP.

YET IT'S ALSO FULL OF WORKS OF REFINED BRILLIANCE AND DEPTH—AND AN AWFUL LOT IN BETWEEN.

EXACTLY THE SAME CAN BE SAID OF THE WEB ITSELF. TEN YEARS AGO, PEOPLE COMPLAINED THAT THERE WAS A LOT OF JUNK ON THE INTERNET, AND SURE ENOUGH, ANY CASUAL SURF QUICKLY CONFIRMED THAT.

JUST THINK ABOUT ART, NOT FROM THE PERSPECTIVE OF A GALLERY BUT FROM A GARAGE SALE. NINETY PERCENT (AT LEAST) IS CRUD. AND THE SAME IS TRUE FOR MUSIC, BOOKS, AND EVERYTHING ELSE.

OBVIOUSLY, THE TERMS "HIGH QUALITY" AND "LOW QUALITY" ARE ENTIRELY SUBJECTIVE, SO ALL OF THESE CRITERIA ARE IN THE EYE OF THE BEHOLDER. ONE PERSON'S "GOOD" COULD EASILY BE ANOTHER'S "BAD"; INDEED, IT ALMOST ALWAYS IS.

THEN ALONG CAME SEARCH ENGINES TO HELP PULL SOME SIGNAL FROM THE NOISE, AND FINALLY, GOOGLE, WHICH TAPS THE WISDOM OF THE CROWD ITSELF AND TURNS A MASS OF INCOHERENCE INTO THE CLOSEST THING TO AN ORACLE THE WORLD HAS EVER SEEN.

THIS IS NOT UNIQUE TO THE WEB—IT'S TRUE EVERYWHERE.

THIS IS WHY NICHES ARE DIFFERENT. ONE PERSON'S NOISE IS ANOTHER'S SIGNAL.

IF A PRODUCER INTENDS SOMETHING TO BE ABSOLUTELY RIGHT FOR ONE AUDIENCE, IT WILL, BY DEFINITION, BE WRONG FOR ANOTHER. THE COMPROMISES NECESSARY TO MAKE SOMETHING APPEAL TO EVERYONE MEAN THAT IT WILL ALMOST CERTAINLY NOT APPEAL PERFECTLY TO ANYONE—THAT'S WHY THEY CALL IT THE LOWEST COMMON DENOMINATOR.

WHEN YOU THINK ABOUT IT, THE WORLD IS ALREADY FULL OF A DIFFERENT KIND OF FILTER.

IN THE SCARCITY DRIVEN MARKETS OF LIMITED SHELVES, SCREENS, AND CHANNELS THAT WE'VE LIVED WITH FOR MOST OF THE PAST CENTURY, ENTIRE INDUSTRIES HAVE BEEN CREATED AROUND FINDING AND PROMOTING THE GOOD STUFF.

MUSIC REVIEWS

MAGAZINES

MOVIE REVIEWS

WEDDING DRESS REVIEWS

MAGAZINES

BY CONTRAST, THE RECOMMENDATIONS AND SEARCH TECHNOLOGIES THAT I'M WRITING ABOUT ARE "POST-FILTERS."

THESE POST-FILTERS FIND THE BEST OF WHAT'S ALREADY OUT THERE IN THEIR AREA OF INTEREST, ELEVATING THE GOOD AND DOWNPLAYING, EVEN IGNORING THE BAD.

THE 80/20 RULE IS OFTEN USED TO EXPLAIN THAT 20 PERCENT OF PRODUCTS ACCOUNT FOR 80 PERCENT OF REVENUES, OR 20 PERCENT OF OUR TIME ACCOUNTS FOR 80 PERCENT OF OUR PRODUCTIVITY, OR ANY NUMBER OF OTHER COMPARISONS THAT ALL SHARE THIS CHARACTERISTIC OF A MINORITY HAVING DISPROPORTIONATE IMPACT.

THE 80/20 RULE IS CHRONICALLY MISUNDERSTOOD, FOR THREE REASONS.

FIRST, IT'S ALMOST NEVER EXACTLY 80/20. MOST OF THE LARGE INVENTORY MARKETS I'VE STUDIED ARE 80/10 OR EVEN LESS (NO MORE THAN 10 PERCENT OF PRODUCTS ACCOUNT FOR 80 PERCENT OF SALES).

IF YOU'RE TROUBLED BY THE FACT THAT 80/10 DOESN'T ADD UP TO 100, YOU'VE DISCOVERED THE SECOND CONFUSING THING ABOUT THE RULE.

80 + 10 = 100??

SKRIT SKRIT

THE 80 EQUALS 100. ONE IS A PERCENTAGE OF PRODUCTS, THE OTHER A PERCENTAGE OF SALES. WORSE, THERE'S NO STANDARD CONVENTION ON HOW TO EXPRESS THE RELATIONSHIP BETWEEN THE TWO, OR WHICH VARIABLE TO HOLD CONSTANT. SAYING A MARKET HAS AN 80/10 SHAPE CAN BE THE SAME AS SAYING IT'S 95/20 (20 PERCENT OF PRODUCTS ACCOUNT FOR 95 PERCENT OF SALES).

FINALLY, THE RULE IS MISUNDERSTOOD BECAUSE, WHILE THE CLASSIC DEFINITION IS ABOUT PRODUCTS AND REVENUES, THE RULE CAN JUST AS EQUALLY BE APPLIED TO PRODUCTS AND PROFITS.

ONE OF THE MOST PERNICIOUS MIS-INTERPRETATIONS IS TO ASSUME THAT THE 80/20 RULE IS AN INVITATION TO CARRY ONLY THE 20 PERCENT OF GOODS THAT ACCOUNT FOR THE MOST SALES.

MANY SEE THE LONG TAIL AS THE DEATH OF THE 80/20 RULE, EVEN THOUGH IT'S ACTUALLY NOTHING OF THE SORT. THE REAL 80/20 RULE IS JUST THE ACKNOWLEDGMENT THAT SOME THINGS WILL SELL A LOT BETTER THAN OTHERS, WHICH IS AS TRUE IN LONG TAIL MARKETS AS IT IS IN TRADITIONAL MARKETS.

WHAT THE LONG TAIL OFFERS, HOWEVER, IS THE ENCOURAGEMENT TO NOT BE DOMINATED BY THE RULE.

EVEN IF 20 PERCENT OF THE PRODUCTS ACCOUNT FOR 80 PERCENT OF THE REVENUE, THAT'S NO REASON NOT TO CARRY THE OTHER 80 PERCENT OF THE PRODUCTS. IN LONG TAIL MARKETS, WHERE THE CARRYING COSTS OF INVENTORY ARE LOW, THE INCENTIVE IS THERE TO CARRY EVERYTHING REGARDLESS OF THE VOLUME OF ITS SALES.

THE 80/20 RULE CHANGES IN THREE WAYS IN LONG TAIL MARKETS:

YOU CAN OFFER MANY MORE PRODUCTS.

BECAUSE IT IS SO MUCH EASIER TO FIND THESE PRODUCTS (THANKS TO RECOMMENDATIONS AND OTHER FILTERS), SALES ARE SPREAD MORE EVENLY BETWEEN HITS AND NICHES.

BECAUSE THE ECONOMICS OF NICHES IS ROUGHLY THE SAME AS HITS, THERE ARE PROFITS TO BE FOUND AT ALL LEVELS OF POPULARITY.

BUILD·A·GNOME

WHILE THE 80/20 RULE IS STILL ALIVE AND WELL, IN A LONG TAIL MARKET IT HAS LOST ITS BITE.

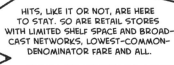

HITS, LIKE IT OR NOT, ARE HERE TO STAY. SO ARE RETAIL STORES WITH LIMITED SHELF SPACE AND BROAD-CAST NETWORKS, LOWEST-COMMON-DENOMINATOR FARE AND ALL.

FOR ALL THE GROWTH IN E-COMMERCE, ONLINE SHOPPING IS STILL LESS THAN 10 PERCENT OF AMERICAN RETAIL, HAVING JUST PASSED CATALOG SHOPPING. EVEN THE BIGGEST BOOSTERS OF ONLINE SHIPPING DON'T EXPECT THAT THEY'LL PASS A QUARTER OF CONSUMER SPENDING FOR DECADES.

WE'RE A GREGARIOUS SPECIES, AND SOMETIMES WE LIKE TO DO THINGS TOGETHER WITH OTHER PEOPLE. THERE'S COMFORT IN NUMBERS, AND SHARED EXPERIENCES BRING US CLOSER.

HITS MAY NOT DOMINATE SOCIETY AND COMMERCE AS MUCH AS THEY DID OVER THE PAST CENTURY, BUT THEY STILL HAVE UNMATCHED IMPACT. AND PART OF THAT IS THEIR ABILITY TO SERVE AS A SOURCE OF COMMON CULTURE AROUND WHICH MORE NARROWLY TARGETED MARKETS CAN FORM.

SUCCESSFUL LONG TAIL AGGREGATORS NEED TO HAVE BOTH HITS AND NICHES.

IF YOU JUST HAVE PRODUCTS AT THE HEAD, YOU FIND THAT VERY QUICKLY YOUR CUSTOMERS WANT MORE AND YOU CAN'T OFFER IT.

IF YOU JUST HAVE THE PRODUCTS AT THE TAIL, YOU FIND THAT CUSTOMERS HAVE NO IDEA WHERE TO START. THEY'RE UNABLE TO GET TRACTION IN THE MARKETPLACE BECAUSE EVERYTHING YOU'RE OFFERING IS UNFAMILIAR TO THEM.

THE IMPORTANCE OF OFFERING THE STUFF AT BOTH THE HEAD AND THE TAIL IS THAT YOU CAN START IN THE WORLD THAT CUSTOMERS ALREADY KNOW: FAMILIAR PRODUCTS THAT TAP INTO AND DEFINE A SPACE.

BEFORE WE BURY THE SHELF, LET US FIRST PRAISE IT.

THE SHELF REFLECTS THE ABSOLUTE STATE OF THE ART IN RETAIL SCIENCE.

THE PRODUCTS ON TODAY'S SUPERMARKET SHELVES ARE PACKAGED AND ARRANGED ACCORDING TO STOCKING ALGORITHMS AND THE PEAKS OF ELASTIC DEMAND CURVES.

TODAY'S RETAIL DISPLAY RACK IS THE HUMAN INTERFACE TO A HIGHLY EVOLVED SUPPLY CHAIN DESIGNED TO MAKE THE MOST OF TIME AND SPACE.

WE ARE IN THE MIDST OF THE BIGGEST EXPLOSION OF VARIETY IN HISTORY. YOU CAN SEE IT ALL AROUND YOU, BUT SOMETIMES A FEW NUMBERS MAKE THE POINT EVEN BETTER.

THERE ARE PRECISELY 19,000 VARIATIONS OF STARBUCKS COFFEE, ACCORDING TO THE ADVERTISING FIRM OMD. IN 2003 ALONE, 26,893 NEW FOOD AND HOUSEHOLD PRODUCTS WERE INTRODUCED, INCLUDING 115 DEODORANTS, 187 BREAKFAST CEREALS, AND 303 WOMEN'S FRAGRANCES.

WHY HAS THERE BEEN SUCH AN EXPLOSION OF VARIETY?

PART OF THE ANSWER IS GLOBALIZATION AND THE HYPEREFFICIENT SUPPLY CHAINS IT BRINGS. MERCHANTS IN ONE COUNTRY CAN NOW PULL FROM A TRULY GLOBAL RANGE OF PRODUCTS.

ANOTHER PART OF THE ANSWER IS DEMOGRAPHICS.

WE'VE HAD A CHANGE FROM "I WANT TO BE NORMAL" TO "I WANT TO BE SPECIAL."

FINALLY, THERE IS THE LONG TAIL ITSELF. THE OVERWHELMING REALITY OF OUR ONLINE AGE IS THAT EVERYTHING CAN BE AVAILABLE. ONLINE RETAILERS OFFER VARIETY ON A SCALE UNIMAGINABLE EVEN A DECADE AGO.

BUT DOES ANYONE NEED THIS MUCH CHOICE? CAN WE HANDLE IT?

THE CONVENTIONAL VIEW IS THAT MORE CHOICE IS BETTER, BECAUSE IT ACKNOWLEDGES THAT PEOPLE ARE DIFFERENT AND ALLOWS THEM TO FIND WHAT'S RIGHT FOR THEM.

BUT IN THE "PARADOX OF CHOICE," AN INFLUENTIAL BOOK PUBLISHED IN 2004, BARRY SCHWARTZ ARGUED THAT TOO MUCH CHOICE IS NOT JUST CONFUSING BUT IS DOWNRIGHT OPPRESSIVE.

HE CITED A NOW FAMOUS STUDY OF CONSUMER BEHAVIOR IN A SUPERMARKET.

IN THE STUDY, RESEARCHERS SET UP A TABLE AT A SPECIALTY FOOD STORE AND OFFERED CUSTOMERS A TASTE OF A RANGE OF JAMS AND A $1 COUPON TO USE AGAINST THE PURCHASE OF ANY SINGLE JAR OF JAM. HALF THE TIME THE TABLE HELD SIX FLAVORS, HALF THE TIME IT OFFERED TWENTY-FOUR.

THE RESULTS WERE CLEAR: 30 PERCENT OF THE CUSTOMERS WHO TASTED FROM THE SMALL SELECTION WENT ON TO BUY A JAR, WHILE JUST 3 PERCENT OF THOSE WHO SAMPLED FROM THE LARGER SELECTION DID.

INTERESTINGLY, THE LARGER SELECTION ATTRACTED MORE TASTERS—60 PERCENT COMPARED TO 40 PERCENT FOR THE SMALLER SELECTION. THEY JUST DIDN'T BUY. THE MORE CHOICE THE RESEARCHERS OFFERED, THE LESS CUSTOMERS BOUGHT, AND THE LESS SATISFIED THEY WERE WITH ANY PURCHASE THEY DID MAKE.

TOO... MANY...CHOICES. WHICH ONE?

THE CUSTOMERS APPEARED TO HAVE BEEN CONFUSED, EVEN OPPRESSED, BY THE ABUNDANCE—WHY SHOULD THEY HAVE TO BECOME AN EXPERT ON JAM VARIETIES TO MAKE A SELECTION WITH CONFIDENCE?

INDECISION AND BUYER'S REMORSE BEGAN TO CLOUD THE PICTURE.

AS AN ANTIDOTE TO THIS POISON OF OUR MODERN AGE, SCHWARTZ RECOMMENDED THAT CONSUMERS WOULD BE HAPPIER IF THEY SETTLED FOR WHAT WAS IN FRONT OF THEM RATHER THAN OBSESSING OVER WHETHER SOMETHING ELSE MIGHT BE BETTER.

I'M SKEPTICAL.

THE ALTERNATIVE TO LETTING PEOPLE CHOOSE IS CHOOSING FOR THEM. THE LESSONS OF A CENTURY OF RETAIL SCIENCE ARE THAT THIS IS NOT WHAT MOST CONSUMERS WANT.

VAST CHOICE IS NOT ALWAYS GOOD, OF COURSE. IT TOO OFTEN FORCES US TO ASK: "WELL, WHAT DO I WANT?" AND INTROSPECTION DOESN'T COME NATURALLY TO ALL.

BUT THE SOLUTION IS NOT TO LIMIT CHOICE, BUT TO ORDER IT SO IT ISN'T OPPRESSIVE.

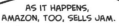

AS IT HAPPENS, AMAZON, TOO, SELLS JAM.

NOT SIX KINDS, OR TWENTY-FOUR KINDS, BUT MORE THAN TWELVE HUNDRED KINDS. YET THERE IS A HUGE DIFFERENCE BETWEEN THE PRESENTATION OF VARIETY IN THE PHYSICAL WORLD AND ONLINE.

IN A BRICKS-AND-MORTAR STORE, PRODUCTS SIT ON THE SHELF WHERE THEY HAVE BEEN PLACED.

IF A CONSUMER DOESN'T KNOW WHAT HE OR SHE WANTS, THE ONLY GUIDE IS WHATEVER MARKETING MATERIAL MAY BE PRINTED ON THE PACKAGE, AND THE ROUGH ASSUMPTION THAT THE PRODUCT OFFERED IN THE GREATEST VOLUME IS PROBABLY THE MOST POPULAR.

TOMMY! STOP TEASING YOUR SISTER!

GET BACK HERE, BILLY!

NEW!

ONLINE, HOWEVER, THE CONSUMER HAS A LOT MORE HELP.

YOU CAN SORT BY PRICE, BY RATINGS, BY DATE, AND BY GENRE. YOU CAN READ CUSTOMER REVIEWS. YOU CAN COMPARE PRICES ACROSS PRODUCTS AND, IF YOU WANT, HEAD OFF TO GOOGLE TO FIND OUT AS MUCH ABOUT THE PRODUCT AS YOU CAN IMAGINE.

THE PROBLEM WITH THE JAM EXPERIMENT IS THAT IT WAS DISORDERED. ALL THE JAMS WERE SHOWN SIMULTANEOUSLY AND TO GUIDE THEM THE CUSTOMERS HAD ONLY THEIR EXISTING KNOWLEDGE OF JAM OR WHATEVER WAS WRITTEN ON THE LABELS.

THAT'S THE PROBLEM ON THE SUPERMARKET SHELF, TOO. ALL YOU HAVE TO GO ON IS YOUR DOMAIN EXPERTISE, WHATEVER BRAND INFORMATION HAS BEEN LODGED IN YOUR BRAIN BY EXPERIENCE OR ADVERTISING, AND THE MARKETING MESSAGES OF THE PACKAGING AND SHELF PLACEMENT.

THE PARADOX OF CHOICE IS SIMPLY AN ARTIFACT OF THE LIMITA-TION OF THE PHYSICAL WORLD, WHERE THE INFORMATION NECESSARY TO MAKE AN INFORMED CHOICE IS LOST.

THE CONVENTIONAL WISDOM WAS RIGHT. MORE CHOICE IS BETTER. BUT NOW WE KNOW THAT VARIETY ALONE IS NOT ENOUGH; WE ALSO NEED INFORMATION ABOUT THAT VARIETY AND WHAT OTHER CONSUMERS BEFORE US HAVE DONE WITH THE SAME CHOICES.

THE LONG TAIL IS NOTHING MORE THAN INFINITE CHOICE.

ABUNDANT, CHEAP DISTRIBUTION MEANS ABUNDANT, CHEAP, AND UNLIMITED VARIETY—AND THAT MEANS THE AUDIENCE TENDS TO DISTRIBUTE AS WIDELY AS THE CHOICE.

FROM THE MAINSTREAM MEDIA AND ENTERTAINMENT INDUSTRY PERSPECTIVE, THIS LOOKS LIKE A BATTLE BETWEEN TRADITIONAL MEDIA AND THE INTERNET.

BUT THE PROBLEM IS THAT ONCE PEOPLE SHIFT THEIR ATTENTION ONLINE, THEY DON'T JUST GO FROM ONE MEDIA OUTLET TO ANOTHER—THEY SIMPLY SCATTER. INFINITE CHOICE EQUALS ULTIMATE FRAGMENTATION.

THIS SHIFT FROM THE GENERIC TO THE SPECIFIC DOESN'T MEAN THE END OF THE EXISTING POWER STRUCTURE OR A WHOLESALE SHIFT TO AN ALL-AMATEUR, LAPTOP CULTURE.

INSTEAD, IT'S SIMPLY A REBALANCING OF THE EQUATIONS, AN EVOLUTION FROM AN "OR" ERA OF HITS OR NICHES (MAINSTREAM CULTURE VS. SUBCULTURES) TO AN "AND" ERA.

TODAY, OUR CULTURE IS INCREASINGLY A MIX OF HEAD AND TAIL, HITS AND NICHES, INSTITUTIONS AND INDIVIDUALS, PROFESSIONALS AND AMATEURS. MASS CULTURE WILL NOT FALL; IT WILL SIMPLY GET LESS MASS. AND NICHE CULTURE WILL GET LESS OBSCURE.

WHETHER WE THINK OF IT THIS WAY OR NOT, EACH OF US BELONGS TO MANY DIFFERENT TRIBES SIMULTANEOUSLY, OFTEN OVERLAPPING, OFTEN NOT.

WE SHARE SOME INTERESTS WITH OUR COLLEAGUES AND SOME WITH OUR FAMILIES, BUT NOT ALL OF OUR INTERESTS. INCREASINGLY, WE HAVE OTHERS WE SHARE THEM WITH, PEOPLE WE HAVE NEVER MET OR EVEN THINK OF AS INDIVIDUALS.

IS A FRAGMENTED CULTURE A BETTER OR WORSE CULTURE?

MANY BELIEVE THAT MASS CULTURE SERVES AS A SORT OF SOCIAL GLUE, KEEPING SOCIETY TOGETHER. BUT IF WE'RE NOW ALL OFF DOING OUR OWN THING, IS THERE STILL A COMMON CULTURE? ARE OUR INTERESTS STILL ALIGNED WITH THOSE OF OUR NEIGHBORS?

A WORLD OF NICHES IS INDEED A WORLD OF ABUNDANT CHOICE, BUT POWERFUL GUIDES IN THE FORM OF RECOMMENDATIONS AND OTHER FILTERS HAVE EMERGED TO ENCOURAGE MORE EXPLORATION, NOT LESS. WE LOAD OUR IPODS WITH MUSIC WE GET FROM OUR FRIENDS, AND OUR TIVOS CEASELESSLY SUGGEST NEW SHOWS WE MIGHT LIKE BASED ON THE WATCHING PATTERNS OF OTHERS.

THE EVIDENCE FROM NETFLIX SUGGESTS THAT WHEN GIVEN THE ABILITY TO PICK ANY MOVIE FROM A SELECTION OF TENS OF THOUSANDS, CUSTOMERS DON'T JUST DIVE INTO THE WORLD WAR II DOCUMENTARY NICHE AND NEVER COME OUT.

BRAP BRAP

INSTEAD, REDISCOVERING CLASSICS ONE MONTH AND GOING ON A SCI-FI BENDER THE NEXT.

MEANWHILE, THE BLOGOSPHERE IS THE GREATEST VECTOR FOR NEW VOICES EVER CREATED. THE CONVENTION OF LINKING TO IDEAS AND INFORMATION OF MERIT, WHEREVER THEY COME FROM, BE IT PROFESSIONAL OR AMATEUR, IS A POWERFUL FORCE OF DIVERSITY.

ANYONE WHO IS READING ONLINE AND NOT ENLARGING THEIR CULTURAL PERSPECTIVE HAS EITHER FOUND SOME REMARKABLY BARREN CORNER OF THE BLOG WORLD OR NEEDS A REFRESHER COURSE IN THE MEANING OF HYPERLINKS.

SINCE NOTHING ON THE WEB IS AUTHORITATIVE, IT'S UP TO YOU TO CONSULT ENOUGH SOURCES SO THAT YOU CAN MAKE UP YOUR OWN MIND.

THIS IS THE END OF SPOON-FED ORTHODOXY AND INFALLIBLE INSTITUTIONS, AND THE RISE OF MASS MOSAICS OF INFORMATION THAT REQUIRE—AND REWARD—INVESTIGATION.

OVER TIME THE POWER OF HUMAN CURIOSITY COMBINED WITH NEAR INFINITE ACCESS TO INFORMATION WILL TEND TO MAKE MOST PEOPLE MORE OPEN-MINDED, NOT LESS.

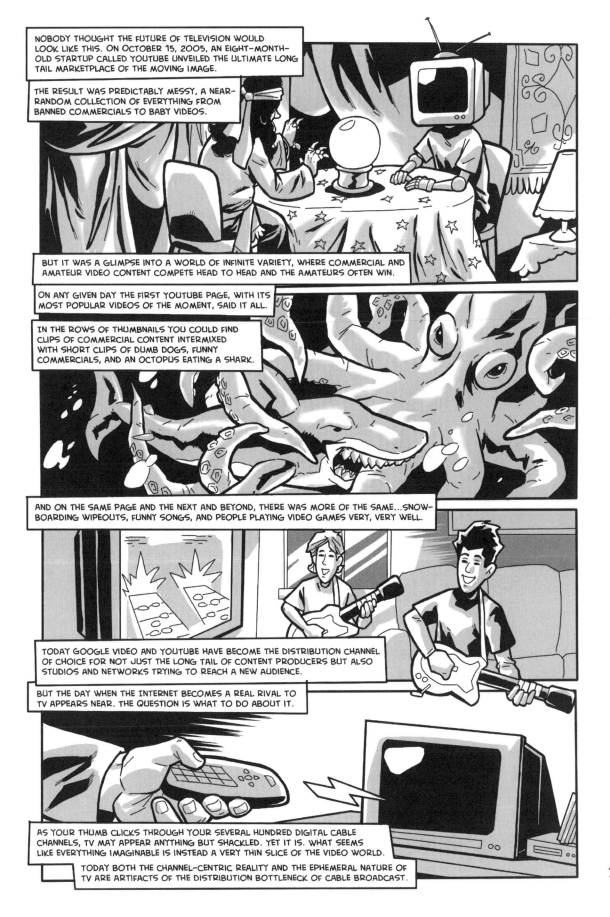

NOBODY THOUGHT THE FUTURE OF TELEVISION WOULD LOOK LIKE THIS. ON OCTOBER 15, 2005, AN EIGHT-MONTH-OLD STARTUP CALLED YOUTUBE UNVEILED THE ULTIMATE LONG TAIL MARKETPLACE OF THE MOVING IMAGE.

THE RESULT WAS PREDICTABLY MESSY, A NEAR-RANDOM COLLECTION OF EVERYTHING FROM BANNED COMMERCIALS TO BABY VIDEOS.

BUT IT WAS A GLIMPSE INTO A WORLD OF INFINITE VARIETY, WHERE COMMERCIAL AND AMATEUR VIDEO CONTENT COMPETE HEAD TO HEAD AND THE AMATEURS OFTEN WIN.

ON ANY GIVEN DAY THE FIRST YOUTUBE PAGE, WITH ITS MOST POPULAR VIDEOS OF THE MOMENT, SAID IT ALL.

IN THE ROWS OF THUMBNAILS YOU COULD FIND CLIPS OF COMMERCIAL CONTENT INTERMIXED WITH SHORT CLIPS OF DUMB DOGS, FUNNY COMMERCIALS, AND AN OCTOPUS EATING A SHARK.

AND ON THE SAME PAGE AND THE NEXT AND BEYOND, THERE WAS MORE OF THE SAME...SNOW-BOARDING WIPEOUTS, FUNNY SONGS, AND PEOPLE PLAYING VIDEO GAMES VERY, VERY WELL.

TODAY GOOGLE VIDEO AND YOUTUBE HAVE BECOME THE DISTRIBUTION CHANNEL OF CHOICE FOR NOT JUST THE LONG TAIL OF CONTENT PRODUCERS BUT ALSO STUDIOS AND NETWORKS TRYING TO REACH A NEW AUDIENCE.

BUT THE DAY WHEN THE INTERNET BECOMES A REAL RIVAL TO TV APPEARS NEAR. THE QUESTION IS WHAT TO DO ABOUT IT.

AS YOUR THUMB CLICKS THROUGH YOUR SEVERAL HUNDRED DIGITAL CABLE CHANNELS, TV MAY APPEAR ANYTHING BUT SHACKLED. YET IT IS. WHAT SEEMS LIKE EVERYTHING IMAGINABLE IS INSTEAD A VERY THIN SLICE OF THE VIDEO WORLD.

TODAY BOTH THE CHANNEL-CENTRIC REALITY AND THE EPHEMERAL NATURE OF TV ARE ARTIFACTS OF THE DISTRIBUTION BOTTLENECK OF CABLE BROADCAST.

TV IS STILL IN THE ERA OF LIMITED SHELF SPACE.

THE GROWTH OF CABLE CAPACITY OVER THE PAST DECADE PALES NEXT TO THE GROWTH IN VIDEO CREATION OVER THE SAME PERIOD AND IN THE SIZE OF THE POTENTIAL MICROAUDIENCES FOR ANYTHING AND EVERYTHING.

OF ALL THE TRADITIONAL MEDIA INDUSTRIES, TELEVISION IS NOW THE INDUSTRY WITH THE GREATEST POTENTIAL TO BE TRANSFORMED BY LONG TAIL FORCES.

HERE'S WHY...

TV PRODUCES MORE CONTENT THAN ANY OTHER MEDIA AND ENTERTAINMENT INDUSTRY. THE AMOUNT OF VIDEO PRODUCED EACH YEAR IS STAGGERING BUT ONLY A TINY FRACTION OF IT IS AVAILABLE TO YOU.

FIRST, THE AVERAGE AMERICAN HOUSEHOLD NOW GETS ONE HUNDRED CHANNELS OF TV.

WHILE THAT SOUNDS LIKE A LOT—IT'S 876,000 HOURS OF VIDEO BROADCAST TO THE AVERAGE HOME EACH YEAR—THAT'S STILL LESS THAN 10 PERCENT OF THE VIDEO THAT'S BROADCAST IN THE UNITED STATES.

IT'S THE END OF THE COUCH POTATO ERA.

WHEN YOU THINK ABOUT IT, IN THE PEAK OF THE NETWORK TV AGE, WE MAY ALL HAVE BEEN WATCHING THE SAME THINGS, BUT WE WERE ALL TOO OFTEN WATCHING THEM BY OURSELVES— "BOWLING ALONE" IN PRIME TIME.

ONLINE TODAY WE'RE DOING DIFFERENT THINGS, BUT ARE MORE LIKELY TO ENCOUNTER OTHER INDIVIDUALS, EITHER BY READING THEIR WRITINGS, CHATTING LIVE, OR JUST FOLLOWING THEIR EXAMPLE.

WHAT WE'VE LOST IN COMMON CULTURE WE'VE MADE UP IN OUR INCREASED EXPOSURE TO OTHER PEOPLE.

TODAY WE'RE NOT SO MUCH FRAGMENTING AS WE ARE RE-FORMING ALONG DIFFERENT DIMENSIONS.

THESE DAYS OUR WATER COOLERS ARE INCREASINGLY VIRTUAL.

GET OUT THERE YA BUM!

HAK HAK

THERE IS NO SHORTAGE OF SMART PEOPLE THINKING ABOUT HOW TV CAN FIND ITS WAY OUT OF ITS CORNER.

BUT IT'S NOT EASY. FOR STARTERS, MOST OF THE NETWORKS ARE CONTENT RENTERS, NOT CONTENT OWNERS. THIS MEANS THAT THE ARCHIVES ARE OFTEN NOT THEIRS TO CAPITALIZE ON.

RIGHTS ARE A TOTAL HAIRBALL, MADE EVEN MORE COMPLICATED BY EXCLUSIVE REGIONAL DISTRIBUTION DEALS AND SYNDICATION OPTIONS.

BUT THERE IS ANOTHER CLASS OF VIDEO, ONE DESIGNED FROM THE START TO BE DISTRIBUTED ON THE INTERNET.

THIS SORT OF VIDEO—THE PRODUCT OF THE SPREAD OF DIGITAL CAMCORDERS AND DESKTOP ANIMATION TOOLS—HAS FEW SUCH LEGAL ENCUMBRANCES.

CREATED FROM SCRATCH TO BE STREAMED FOR FREE ONLINE, IT'S ALREADY PROVING TO BE THE RICHEST, MOST ENTREPRENEURIAL SOURCE OF PROGRAMMING FOR A POST-BROADCAST AGE.

THE OTHER FORM OF VIDEO THAT WILL BE TRANSFORMED IN A LONG TAIL WORLD IS MOVIES.

THERE, TOO, WE'VE SEEN DISRUPTIVE CHANGE BEFORE. ONE OF THE GREATEST SHIFTS FROM MASS TO NICHE CULTURE HAPPENED IN THE EARLY 1980'S WITH THE INTRODUCTION OF THE VCR AND, MORE IMPORTANT, THE VIDEO RENTAL STORE.

BEFORE THEN, THE SELECTION OF FILMS AVAILABLE TO A MIDDLE-CLASS AMERICAN ON ANY GIVEN NIGHT WAS THE THREE TO FOUR MOVIES PLAYING ON BROADCAST TV, PLUS WHATEVER LOCAL THEATERS HAPPENED TO BE FEATURING.

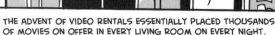

THE ADVENT OF VIDEO RENTALS ESSENTIALLY PLACED THOUSANDS OF MOVIES ON OFFER IN EVERY LIVING ROOM ON EVERY NIGHT.

THE RESULT WAS A TRANSITION FROM PUSHED MEDIA (WHETHER PUSHED ONTO THE AIRWAVES OR INTO THE LOCAL THEATERS) TO PULLED MEDIA. CONSUMERS WERE SUDDENLY EMPOWERED TO SUMMON MOVIES WITH A DEGREE OF WHIM AND FREEDOM THAT, JUST A FEW DECADES BEFORE, WALT DISNEY HIMSELF COULDN'T POSSIBLY HAVE IMAGINED.

WHAT THE VCR AND VIDEO RENTAL STORE HINTED AT WAS THE RISE OF THE AGE OF INFINITE CHOICE. THOSE STORES INCREASED THE AVAILABLE SELECTION OF MOVIES ON ANY GIVEN SATURDAY NIGHT A HUNDREDFOLD.

CABLE TV ALSO INCREASED TELEVISION CHOICE A HUNDREDFOLD.

TODAY, NETFLIX INCREASES IT A THOUSANDFOLD. THE INTERNET WILL INCREASE IT A GAZILLIONFOLD.

THE SECRET TO CREATING A THRIVING LONG TAIL BUSINESS CAN BE SUMMARIZED IN TWO IMPERATIVES:

SEE YOU TOMORROW, GLADYS.

MAKE EVERYTHING AVAILABLE.

HELP ME FIND IT.

THE FIRST IS EASIER SAID THAN DONE. FEWER THAN A DOZEN OF THE 6,000 FILMS SUBMITTED TO THE SUNDANCE FILM FESTIVAL EACH YEAR ARE PICKED UP FOR DISTRIBUTION, BUT MOST OF THE REST OF THEM CANNOT LEGALLY BE SHOWN OUTSIDE OF A FESTIVAL BECAUSE THEIR MUSIC RIGHTS HAVE NOT BEEN CLEARED. LIKEWISE FOR MOST TV PROGRAMMING IN THE NETWORKS' ARCHIVES: IT'S TOO EXPENSIVE TO CLEAR THE DVD OR STREAMING DISTRIBUTION RIGHTS TO THE MUSIC.

SIMILAR RIGHTS ISSUES ALSO KEEP CLASSIC MUSIC AND VIDEO GAMES UNDER LOCK AND KEY. UNTIL WE HAVE SOME WAY TO CLEAR THE RIGHTS TO ALL THE TITLES IN ALL THE BACK CATALOGS, LEGAL RESTRICTIONS WILL CONTINUE TO BE THE PRIMARY BARRIER TO GROWING THE LONG TAIL.

THE SECOND NECESSARY ELEMENT IS MOVING MORE QUICKLY. FROM COLLABORATIVE FILTERING TO USER RATINGS, SMART AGGREGATORS ARE USING RECOMMENDATIONS TO DRIVE DEMAND DOWN THE LONG TAIL.

PUSH PULL

THIS IS THE DIFFERENCE BETWEEN PUSH AND PULL, BETWEEN BROADCAST AND PERSONALIZED TASTE.

NOW THAT YOU'VE GOT THE BIG PICTURE, HERE ARE NINE RULES OF SUCCESSFUL LONG TAIL AGGREGATORS:

43

RULE 1: MOVE INVENTORY WAY IN....OR WAY OUT. ELIMINATING ATOMS OR THE CONSTRAINTS OF THE BROADCAST SPECTRUM IS A POWERFUL WAY TO REDUCE COSTS, ENABLING ENTIRELY NEW MARKETS OF NICHES.

RULE 2: LET CUSTOMERS DO THE WORK: "PEER-PRODUCTION" CREATED EBAY, WIKIPEDIA, CRAIGSLIST, MYSPACE AND PROVIDED NETFLIX WITH HUNDREDS OF THOUSANDS OF MOVIE REVIEWS.

RULE 3: ONE DISTRIBUTION METHOD DOESN'T FIT ALL. IF YOU FOCUS ON DISTRIBUTING TO JUST ONE CUSTOMER GROUP, YOU RISK LOSING THE OTHERS.

RULE 4: ONE PRODUCT DOESN'T FIT ALL.

ONCE UPON A TIME, THERE WAS ONE WAY TO BUY MUSIC: THE CD ALBUM. NOW CONSIDER THE CHOICE YOU HAVE ONLINE: ALBUM, INDIVIDUAL TRACK, RINGTONE, FREE THIRTY-SECOND SAMPLE, MUSIC VIDEO, REMIX, SAMPLE OF SOMEBODY ELSE'S REMIX, STREAMED OR DOWNLOADED, ALL IN ANY NUMBER OF FORMATS AND SAMPLING RATES.

RULE 5: ONE PRICE DOESN'T FIT ALL.

DIFFERENT PEOPLE ARE WILLING TO PAY DIFFERENT PRICES FOR ANY NUMBER OF REASONS, FROM HOW MUCH MONEY THEY HAVE TO HOW MUCH TIME THEY HAVE. BUT JUST AS THERE'S OFTEN ROOM FOR JUST ONE VERSION OF A PRODUCT IN TRADITIONAL MARKETS, THERE'S OFTEN ROOM FOR ONLY ONE PRICE, OR AT LEAST ONE PRICE AT A TIME. IN MARKETS WITH ROOM FOR ABUNDANT VARIETY, HOWEVER, VARIABLE PRICING CAN BE A POWERFUL TECHNIQUE TO MAXIMIZE THE VALUE OF A PRODUCT AND THE SIZE OF THE MARKET.

44

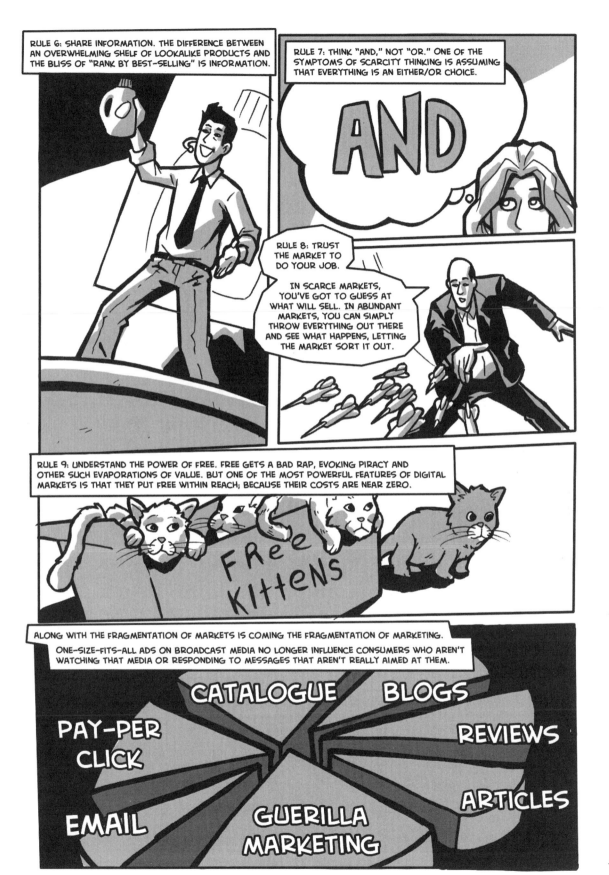

RULE 6: SHARE INFORMATION. THE DIFFERENCE BETWEEN AN OVERWHELMING SHELF OF LOOKALIKE PRODUCTS AND THE BLISS OF "RANK BY BEST-SELLING" IS INFORMATION.

RULE 7: THINK "AND," NOT "OR." ONE OF THE SYMPTOMS OF SCARCITY THINKING IS ASSUMING THAT EVERYTHING IS AN EITHER/OR CHOICE.

AND

RULE 8: TRUST THE MARKET TO DO YOUR JOB.

IN SCARCE MARKETS, YOU'VE GOT TO GUESS AT WHAT WILL SELL. IN ABUNDANT MARKETS, YOU CAN SIMPLY THROW EVERYTHING OUT THERE AND SEE WHAT HAPPENS, LETTING THE MARKET SORT IT OUT.

RULE 9: UNDERSTAND THE POWER OF FREE. FREE GETS A BAD RAP, EVOKING PIRACY AND OTHER SUCH EVAPORATIONS OF VALUE. BUT ONE OF THE MOST POWERFUL FEATURES OF DIGITAL MARKETS IS THAT THEY PUT FREE WITHIN REACH; BECAUSE THEIR COSTS ARE NEAR ZERO.

FRee KiTTeNS

ALONG WITH THE FRAGMENTATION OF MARKETS IS COMING THE FRAGMENTATION OF MARKETING.

ONE-SIZE-FITS-ALL ADS ON BROADCAST MEDIA NO LONGER INFLUENCE CONSUMERS WHO AREN'T WATCHING THAT MEDIA OR RESPONDING TO MESSAGES THAT AREN'T REALLY AIMED AT THEM.

CATALOGUE BLOGS

PAY-PER CLICK REVIEWS

ARTICLES

EMAIL GUERILLA MARKETING

NOTHING BEATS WORD-OF-MOUTH, AND AS WE'VE SEEN, THE WEB IS THE GREATEST WORD-OF-MOUTH AMPLIFIER THE WORLD HAS EVER SEEN.

NO COMPANY CAN CREATE ENOUGH TARGETED MESSAGES TO SUIT EVERY POTENTIAL NICHE WHERE THERE MIGHT BE DEMAND FOR WHAT THEY SELL.

INSTEAD, THE BEST WAY TO MARKET TO LONG TAIL CONSUMERS IS TO FIND OUT WHO IS INFLUENCING THEM AND FOCUS YOUR ENERGIES THERE. THAT STARTS WITH DOING LESS MESSAGING AND MORE LISTENING.

THERE ARE DOZENS OF FREE TOOLS ONLINE THAT CAN TELL YOU WHAT PEOPLE ARE SAYING ABOUT YOUR BRAND AND WHICH OF THOSE PEOPLE HAVE THE MOST INFLUENCE.

TECHNORATI FILTERS (OR GOOGLE ALERTS): YOU CAN SET THESE UP TO TELL YOU ANYTIME A SITE ONLINE LINKS TO A URL YOU SPECIFY OR USES A TERM YOU DEFINE.

SOCIAL NETWORKS: ONE OF THE POWERFUL THINGS ABOUT SITES SUCH AS FACEBOOK IS THAT YOU CAN SEARCH IT FOR BRAND OR PRODUCT MENTIONS AND THEN ANALYZE THE CONTEXT...WHO'S TALKING ABOUT THE PRODUCT, WHAT THEY ARE SAYING, AND WHOM THEY INFLUENCE.

GOOGLE TRENDS: THIS ALLOWS YOU TO SEE HOW OFTEN A PHRASE OR PRODUCT IS BEING SEARCHED FOR, AND COMPARE IT BOTH OVER TIME AND AGAINST OTHER TERMS.

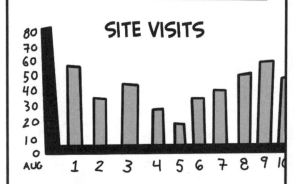

SITE VISITS

RESPONDING TO BLOGGERS IS EASIER IN THEORY, BUT NO LESS DELICATE AND TIME CONSUMING IN PRACTICE.

AGAIN, IT STARTS WITH LISTENING (DESIGNATE SOMEONE TO MONITOR THE FEEDS) AND THEN FIGURING OUT WHEN AND HOW TO RESPOND. IF A BLOGGER PRAISES A COMPANY OR PRODUCT, AN EMAIL OF THANKS IS OFTEN VERY APPRECIATED AND CAN CREATE A LASTING EVANGELIST.

CRITICISM IS TRICKIER. AGAIN, SOME SORT OF RESPONSE IS BETTER THAN NONE, IN PART BECAUSE IT SHOWS THE BLOGGER RESPECT WHICH CAN GO A LONG WAY TOWARD DEFUSING A SITUATION.

BLOG CONVENTION IS TO DO THINGS IN PUBLIC, SO A RESPONSE IN THE COMMENTS, WHERE EVERYONE CAN READ IT, OFTEN PAYS GREATER DIVIDENDS THAN A PRIVATE EMAIL. AND IDEALLY THAT RESPONSE WILL COME FROM SOMEONE OTHER THAN A PR PERSON.

FUNDAMENTALLY SOCIAL MEDIA IS A PEER-TO-PEER MEDIUM; BLOGGERS WOULD RATHER HEAR FROM SOMEONE DOING SOMETHING COOL THAN FROM THE PAID PROMOTIONAL REPRESENTATIVE FOR THAT PERSON.

THE PROBLEM IS THAT THE PEOPLE DOING THAT COOL STUFF ARE BUSY, WHICH IS WHY THEY PAY PR PEOPLE TO DO THE OUTREACH FOR THEM IN THE FIRST PLACE.

MOST PRODUCTS WILL BE SOLD OFFLINE, MUCH AS THEY ALWAYS WERE. BUT IN THE YEARS TO COME, MORE AND MORE PRODUCTS WILL BE MARKETED ONLINE, TAKING ADVANTAGE OF THE ABILITY OF WEB METHODS TO FINE-SLICE CONSUMER GROUPS AND INFLUENCE WORD-OF-MOUTH MORE EFFECTIVELY THAN EVER BEFORE.

COMMON MISPERCEPTION IS THAT THE LONG TAIL PREDICTS THE END OF HITS. NOT SO.

WHAT'S DEAD IS THE MONOPOLY OF THE HIT.

HERE'S A START AT A CURRICULUM FOR SUCH IN-HOUSE SOCIAL MEDIA COACHING.

-WHO'S INFLUENTIAL IN OUR SPACE (AND HOW WE KNOW)
-WHAT/WHO INFLUENCES THEM
-EFFECTIVE BLOGGING
-THE ART OF BEGGING FOR LINKS
-STUNTS, CONTESTS, GIMMICKS, MEMES, AND OTHER LINK BAIT
-SHARING VERSUS OVERSHARING

FORGET THE WEB AS A MARKETPLACE OF PRODUCTS, AND INSTEAD THINK OF IT AS A MARKETPLACE OF OPINION. IT'S THE GREAT LEVELER OF MARKETING. IT ALLOWS FOR NICHE PRODUCTS TO GET GLOBAL ATTENTION.

MARKETING

THERE ARE ESSENTIALLY THREE KINDS OF HITS.

AUTHENTIC TOP-DOWN HITS; PRODUCTS THAT ARE EXCELLENT AND RESONATE WITH A BROAD AUDIENCE. THESE START BIG AND STAY BIG.

SYNTHETIC TOP-DOWN HITS; LAME PRODUCTS THAT ARE MARKETED WITHIN AN INCH OF THEIR LIFE, SUCCESSFULLY GETTING LOTS OF PEOPLE TO TRY THEM EVEN THOUGH THEY'RE PROBABLY SORRY THEY DID. THESE START BIG BUT QUICKLY PLUMMET.

AND BOTTOM-UP HITS THAT RISE ON WORD OF MOUTH AND GRASSROOTS SUPPORT. THESE START SMALL AND GET BIG.

I THINK AUTHENTIC HITS WILL CONTINUE TO DO WELL. GRASSROOTS HITS WILL DO EVEN BETTER, SINCE THE WEB IS THE GREATEST WORD-OF-MOUTH AMPLIFIER EVER CREATED. BUT SYNTHETIC HITS WILL SUFFER, AS THE CONSUMERS SPREAD THE WORD OF THEIR SUCKTITUDE FASTER THAN EVER.

IN A LONG TAIL WORLD MANY TOP-DOWN HITS GET SMALLER BUT EVEN MORE BOTTOM-UP HITS GET BIGGER. IT'S NOT THE END OF THE HIT—IT'S THE RISE OF A NEW KIND OF HIT.

ANOTHER COMMON QUESTION WAS WHETHER THE THEORY MEANT THAT OBSCURE PRODUCERS COULD NOW EXPECT TO GET RICH. SADLY, IT'S NOT AS SIMPLE AS THAT.

48

FIRST, LET'S REVIEW WHAT THIS TWO-PART THEORY ACTUALLY SAYS.

IF YOU CAN DRAMATICALLY LOWER THE COST OF PRODUCTION AND DISTRIBUTION, YOU CAN OFFER FAR MORE VARIETY...

...AND GIVEN MORE VARIETY AND THE TOOLS TO EASILY ORGANIZE IT FOR INDIVIDUAL TASTE, PEOPLE WILL INCREASINGLY REVEL IN THEIR DIFFERENCES RATHER THAN SETTLING FOR THEIR COMMONALITIES AS IN TRADITIONAL BLOCKBUSTER CULTURE.

THERE ARE THREE BASIC TYPES OF PARTICIPANTS IN LONG TAIL MARKETS:

CONSUMERS.

AGGREGATORS.

AND PRODUCERS.

FOR CONSUMERS, THE EFFECT IS LARGELY CULTURAL. PEOPLE HAVE MORE CHOICE, SO INDIVIDUAL TASTE IS INCREASINGLY SATISFIED EVEN IF THE EFFECT IS AN INCREASINGLY FRAGMENTED CULTURE.

FOR AGGREGATORS, THE EFFECT IS LARGELY ECONOMIC. IT'S NEVER BEEN EASIER TO ASSEMBLE VAST VARIETY AND CREATE TOOLS FOR ORGANIZING IT, FROM SEARCH TO RECOMMENDATIONS.

ACTION!

FOR PRODUCERS, THE EFFECT IS LARGELY NON-ECONOMIC. FOR PRODUCERS, LONG TAIL BENEFITS ARE NOT PRIMARILY ABOUT DIRECT REVENUES.

49

50

About the Author

CHRIS ANDERSON, Editor in Chief, Wired magazine

Anderson took the helm of *Wired* in 2001 and has led the magazine to eleven National Magazine Award nominations since, winning the prestigious top prize for general excellence in 2005, 2007 and 2009. He is the author of the New York Times bestsellers *The Long Tail* and *FREE: The Future of Radical Price*, both of which are based on influential articles published in Wired.

He is also founder of Booktour.com, a free online service that connects authors on tour with audiences (Amazon.com took a stake in the company in 2009), and of 3D Robotics, an open source robotics company. He was named in April 2007 to the "*Time* 100," the news magazine's list of the 100 most influential men and women in the world. He previously was at *The Economist*, where he served as U.S. business editor, Asia business editor and technology editor. Anderson's media career began at the two premier science journals, *Nature* and *Science*, where he served in several editorial capacities.

Anderson holds a Bachelor of Science degree in Physics from George Washington University and studied Quantum Mechanics and Science Journalism at the University of California at Berkeley.

About the Artist

At six years old, **Shane Clester** realized that most people aren't happy with their jobs. Even as he drew robots just to see if he could, he decided at that young age that he would turn his artistic play into work. As Shane grew older and studied the nuances of art, his initial excitement evolved into fascination. He was compelled by the replication of life through seemingly limited tools, and embarked on a quest to learn technical proficiency. In the early 2000s, Shane studied briefly under Jim Garrison, well-known for his art anatomy and technical skills. Shane then relocated from Arizona to California, where he learned a powerful lesson: You have to study to be an artist, and then you have to learn the business of being an artist.

Shane discovered that he needed to sell himself before he could sell a product. Over the course of the next several years, he broadened his portfolio to include youth-oriented art and comic books, and sourced clients by attending conferences and book fairs. Some of his clients have included leading comic book publisher IDW, Hasbro, Scholastic, Macmillan, and Times of London. Shane is currently a staff artist for Writers of the Round Table Inc. Of his many projects, Shane is particularly proud of *Skate Farm: Volume 2*, a graphic novel he produced, *Mi Barrio*, a comic book adaptation of Robert Renteria's *From the Barrio to the Board Room*, Larry Winget's *Shut Up, Stop Whining & Get a Life* and a comic book adaptation of *Art of War*. He is currently working on Marshall Goldsmith's *What Got You Here Won't Get You There*, and an adaptation of Machiavelli's *The Prince*, both for Round Table Comics.

Look for these other titles from SmarterComics and Writers of the Round Table Press:

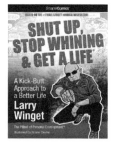

Shut Up, Stop Whining & Get a Life from SmarterComics
by Larry Winget Illustrated by Shane Clester

Internationally renowned success philosopher, business speaker, and humorist, Larry Winget offers advice that flies in the face of conventional self-help. He believes that the motivational speakers and self-help gurus seem to have forgotten that the operative word in self-help is "self." That is what makes this comic so different. *Shut Up, Stop Whining & Get a Life from SmarterComics* forces all responsibility for every aspect of your life right where it belongs—on you. For that reason, this book will make you uncomfortable. Winget won't let you escape to the excuses that we all find so comforting. The only place you are allowed to go to place the blame for everything that has ever happened to you is to the mirror. The last place most of us want to go.

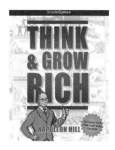

Think and Grow Rich from SmarterComics
by Napoleon Hill Illustrated by Bob Byrne

Think and Grow Rich has sold over 30 million copies and is regarded as the greatest wealth-building guide of all time. Read this comic version and cut to the heart of the message! Written at the advice of millionaire Andrew Carnegie, the book summarizes ideas from over 500 rich and successful people on how to achieve your dreams and get rich doing it. You'll learn money-making secrets - not only what to do but how - laid out in simple steps.

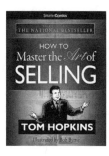

How to Master the Art of Selling from SmarterComics
by Tom Hopkins Illustrated by Bob Byrne

With over one million copies sold in its original version, *How to Master the Art of Selling from SmarterComics* motivates and educates readers to deliver superior sales. After failing during the first six months of his career in sales, Tom Hopkins discovered and applied the very best sales techniques, then earned more than one million dollars in just three years. What turned Tom Hopkins around? The answers are revealed in *How to Master the Art of Selling from SmarterComics*, as Tom explains to readers what the profession of selling is really about and how to succeed beyond their imagination.

The Art of War from SmarterComics
by Sun Tzu Illustrated by Shane Clester

As true today as when it was written, *The Art of War* is a 2,500-year-old classic that is required reading in modern business schools. Penned by the ancient Chinese philosopher and military general Sun Tzu, it reveals how to succeed in any conflict. Read this comic version, and cut to the heart of the message!

Overachievement from SmarterComics
by John Eliot, PH.D. Illustrated by Nathan Lueth

In *Overachievement*, Dr. Eliot offers the rest of us the counterintuitive and unconventional concepts that have been embraced by the Olympic athletes, business moguls, top surgeons, salesmen, financial experts, and rock stars who have turned to him for performance enhancement advice. To really ratchet up your performance, you'll need to change the way you think about becoming exceptional-and that means truly being an exception, abnormal by the standards of most, and loving it. Eliot will teach you that overachieving means thriving under pressure-welcoming it, enjoying it, and making it work to your advantage.

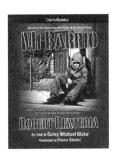

Mi Barrio from SmarterComics
by Robert Renteria as told to Corey Michael Blake
Illustrated by Shane Clester

"Don't let where you came from dictate who you are, but let it be part of who you become." These are the words of successful Latino entrepreneur Robert Renteria who began life as an infant sleeping in a dresser drawer. This poignant and often hard-hitting comic memoir traces Robert's life from a childhood of poverty and abuse in one of the poorest areas of East Los Angeles, to his proud emergence as a business owner and civic leader today.

For more information, please visit www.smartercomics.com

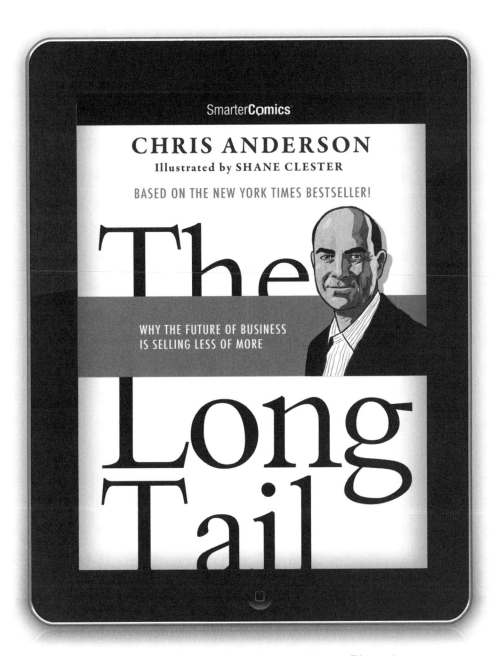

The Long Tail and other SmarterComics™ books
are available for download on the iPad and other devices.

www.smartercomics.com

SmarterComics™

The book that inspired the comic...

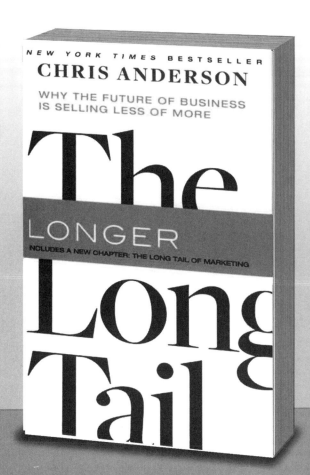

Available everywhere books are sold.